The Tallis Psalter
Psalms and Anthems
Canticles, Preces and Responses

EDITED BY DAVID SKINNER

ISBN 978-1-78305-016-1

Visit Hal Leonard Online at
www.halleonard.com

World headquarters, contact:
Hal Leonard
7777 West Bluemound Road
Milwaukee, WI 53213
Email: info@halleonard.com

In Europe, contact:
Hal Leonard Europe Ltd.
1 Red Place
London W1K 6PL
Email: info@halleonardeurope.com

In Australia, contact:
Hal Leonard Australia Pty. Ltd.
4 Lentara Court
Cheltenham, Victoria, 3192 Australia
Email: info@halleonard.com.au

Project Management by Jonathan Wikeley.
Music Setting by Paul Ewers.

Cover Image: Thomas Tallis's 'Ordinal' from *The Whole Book of Psalms Translated into English Metre*, Corpus Christi College Library, Cambridge, SP.I f. zzi r. Reproduced by kind permission of the Master and Fellows of Corpus Christi College, Cambridge.

Printed in the EU.

Contents

for the Choir of Sidney Sussex College, Cambridge

PREFACE

THOMAS TALLIS lived and worked during the most turbulent years in English ecclesiastical history, and produced music under four Tudor monarchs: Henry VIII, Edward VI, Mary I and Elizabeth I. He was a composer of the Reformation, and for centuries has been known as the Father of English Church Music.

Much has been learned about the lives of early-Tudor composers in recent decades, but little is known of Tallis's early life and career. The estimated year of his birth, 1505, though long accepted, is based on little substance. He first appears as organist of Dover Priory in 1531, but the earliest source of his music, a single Medius part-book (London, British Library, MS Harley 1709), based on its content, can date no earlier than the mid 1520s; it contains what is generally thought to be Tallis's earliest surviving work, *Salve intemerata virgo*. But possibly earlier still is *Ave Dei patris filia* which shows signs of being a student work: it is rather more archaic and is indeed closely modelled on a setting of the same text by the great Dr Robert Fayrfax (d. 1521). This begs the question of whether Tallis, who died in 1585, was born earlier than previously thought. Tallis's career at Dover Priory, Watham Abbey, Canterbury, the Chapel Royal and elsewhere is well documented and does not need to be rehearsed here. What is important to emphasise is his place in the history of English church music, as demonstrated in the variety of the contents of this volume.

With the demise of Latin services, of saintly images in stained glass, of colourful wall paintings of the saints and scriptural scenes, came also the end of an unbroken musical tradition which had evolved into some of the highest art forms of late medieval times: the festal Mass, Magnificat and Votive antiphons. Tallis, as a young man, was a master of these and more, and seems to have learned much from earlier generations. Indeed, his pre-Reformation works are typical of the post Eton-Choirbook tradition of large-scale, wide-canvas and florid compositional style. The function of this music is clear: it served to adorn the liturgy, providing a meditative backdrop for prayer.

With the Edwardine Reformation came the stripping of the altars, white-washing of walls, smashing of stained glass, and, most notably, a liturgy in English recited by priests facing an understanding congregation rather than separated from them by a rood screen and a language barrier. The stacks of Latin liturgical books were swept away and replaced by a single, slimline book in English: *The Book of Common Prayer*. The Prayer Book did not give composers instructions as to how to compose for this new liturgy, but it was clear that the old florid and monumental constructions, with texts in Latin, were no longer acceptable. The oft-quoted injunctions from Lincoln Cathedral from 1548 are quite explicit:

The choir shall henceforth sing or say no anthems of our Lady or other saints, but only of our Lord, and them not in Latin but choosing out the best and most sounding to Christian religion, that they shall turn the same into English, setting thereunto a plain and distinct note, for every syllable one. They shall sing them and none other.

It is clear from Tallis's surviving music for the new English rite that he took these injunctions to heart; he was certainly one of the few mid-16th-century English composers to lead the way in reinventing English composition. In his English anthems, Tallis employed a number of compositional devices, already mastered on the Continent, to enhance the intelligibility of the literary text. These included homophony, close imitation and antiphonal writing, and the majority of anthems are constructed in ABB form so that repetition aids in the absorption of the texts. Music had now become an almost nakedly didactic force, akin to a sermon or moral tale. The medieval offices, too, were compressed: the lesser offices were abolished and the Greater Offices combined into Matins and Evensong. That is why the Vespers and Compline canticles (Magnificat and Nunc dimittis, respectively) are sung during the single office of Evensong in the Anglican liturgy.

Despite Tallis's masterful hand at composing Latin church music, for centuries he was chiefly known for a few works in English. It is thought that Tallis's reception from the 17th century onwards was largely based on those works published by John Barnard in 1641, namely a few of Tallis's Latin motets 'Englished', such as 'I call and cry unto thee' (= *Salvator mundi*) and, most notably, his Morning and Evening Service in the Dorian mode (also known as his Short Service). Such was their popularity of these that by 1840 a 'Tallis Day' was instituted at Westminster Abbey on or close to the feast of St Simon and St Jude (28 October), which then became an annual event (see Suzanne Cole, *Thomas Tallis and his Music in Victorian England*, Boydell Press, 2008). The main musical event at these celebrations was a performance of the Dorian Service. One newspaper report from *The Standard* (Saturday, 29 October, 1842), claimed that the day was actually the 'anniversary of the birthday of Thomas Tallis', although there is no evidence to substantiate this. However, it is perhaps relevant to note that among 'the numerous and respectable congregation' with 'several of the leading musical professors' was the founder of this publishing house, Mr Novello.

The Tallis Psalter

While the Dorian Service, English anthems, and Preces and Responses have variously found their way into modern editions, Tallis's psalm tunes have never been published with all of Matthew Parker's verses so that a liturgical performance might be possible. Parker, born in 1504 and therefore a near contemporary of Tallis, was appointed chaplain to Anne Boleyn in 1535; in the same year the queen presented him to the deanery of the collegiate church at Stoke-by-Clare. In 1544 he was elected Master of his old college of Corpus Christi in Cambridge, to which he was eventually to leave his extensive and impressive library of manuscripts, books and papers. Parker was elected Archbishop of Canterbury early in Elizabeth's reign and held that position until his death in 1575.

According to his autobiographical journal, Parker completed 'a metrical version of the Psalter into the vulgar tongue' on 6 August 1557, and the publication was registered with the Company of Stationers in 1567 or 1568. At the end of the Psalter, Tallis provided harmonisations of eight tunes on each of the church modes in order to show how Parker's metrical psalms might be set to music. He also included a tune and harmonisation for the *Veni Creator* ('Come Holy Ghost'), known as Tallis's 'Ordinal' as liturgically the hymn was variously sung at solemn functions, including the ordination of priests.

Apart from the Ordinal, each tune accommodates two verses which aptly suits modern liturgical performance, the first two verses and doxology being performed full, while the odd verses are performed by 'decani' and the even by 'cantoris', as directed in this edition (although, of course, either side of the stalls can lead the odd verses).

The characterisations of the eight tunes are derived from a longstanding medieval tradition of attributing particular affective qualities to the eight plainchant modes:

The first is meeke: deuout to see
The second is sad: in maiesty
The third doth rage: and roughly brayth
The fourth doth fawne: and flattry playth
The fyfth delighteth: and laugheth the more
The sixt bewayleth: it weepeth full sore
The seuenth tredeth stoute: in froward race
The eyghte goeth milde: in modest pace

Following these is a short preface by the author (presumably Tallis himself) providing the following performance instruction: *The Tenor of these partes be for the people when they will syng alone, the other parts, put for greater queers* [choirs], *or to suche as will syng or play them priuatelye.* As the music is printed in parts, any instrumental accompaniment would seem not to involve keyboards, but lutes, recorders or viols, or any suitable consort instrument of the time.

Changes in the spelling, pronunciation and vocabulary of English since the time of Parker and Tallis require certain alterations to the verbal texts of the Psalter if the settings are to be performed by choirs with neither the time or resources to explore a reconstructed Tudor pronunciation. For this edition, the spelling of words still employed in current English usage has been brought into accord with modern custom (so 'day' for 'daie', 'affairs' for 'affayres'). Consonantal use of 'u' has been normalised (so 'devout' for 'deuout'). The process of normalisation sometimes requires convenience to be set above the preservation of a rhyme, as when the obsolete form 'hond' is normalised to 'hand', losing the rhyme with 'fond'. (There are other places where changes in pronunciation have blurred what were once acceptable rhymes, such as 'threat'/'beat'). In some places one has no choice but to retain an archaic word, and glosses for these have been provided on the page as they have for words, such as 'sad', whose senses in early-modern English might be misleading.

Singers should be aware that this is not lofty poetry, nor was it ever intended to be. The general manner, and rhythmic style, is often that of the popular narrative romances, and the sense is sometimes strained.

Performance Notes

The majority of Tallis's English church music was probably originally conceived for a choir of boy 'means', tenors, baritones and basses. *Blessed be those that are undefiled*, being the only anthem written with pre-Reformation scoring of SATBarB with a wide range from low bass F to top treble G, is one exception. *If ye love me* and *Hear the voice and prayer* are designated 'for men' (i.e. TTBarB), however both have been transposed up for modern SATB performance along with the rest of the works in this collection. There was no pitch standard in the 16th century, so singers should feel free to transpose appropriately. Slurs in the Psalter, which is printed here in short-score format, are editorial and used only to clarify text underlay, which has been standardised according to mid-16th-century convention without further comment. Only *A new commandment* survives in a defective state, and the bass part has been reconstructed by the editor. Tallis's style is so logical that the missing part practically writes itself, and other editors have come to the same or similar conclusions.

Prefatory staves are provided for each work. These give the original clef and first sounding note; rests are not provided. Some explanation should be given about prefatory staves in the Psalter. In the mid 16th century natural signs were often expressed with a sharp. John Day, the printer of Parker's Psalter, did not possess the type which allowed a sharp to be placed on a space, so the nearest line to the B would be used instead. This leads to some confusion when a B natural is expressed within a C clef (e.g., in Tune 3 the Contratenor and Tenor, respectively, have sharps to A and C). I am most grateful to Dr John Milsom for this information.

It is suggested that all works be sung *a cappella*. Certainly there are a number of organ books that contain reductions of many of Tallis's English works, but these date from several decades after their composition and even after the composer's death, so such accompaniment was presumably for rehearsal or for choirs whose forces were inadequate. No such attempt has been made here to follow the reductions in the organ books, but a keyboard reduction for each has been provided should it prove useful in rehearsal.

All works in this edition are available on-line at their original notated pitch and scoring, and may be downloaded at **www.hybridpublications.com**, code **WB559**.

Acknowledgements

The editor is grateful to a number of colleagues and friends who assisted in the publication of this volume. In particular he would like to thank Dr Christopher de Hamel, Parker Librarian at Corpus Christi College, Cambridge, and Professor Christopher Page, who so kindly assisted in the modernisation and interpretation of Parker's poetry. He would also like to express his gratitude to the Choir of Sidney Sussex College, Cambridge, who, during Lent Term 2013, sang through the entire contents of this volume, and it is to them that this book is dedicated.

In keeping with rhymed texts, it is perhaps worth concluding with Tallis's epitaph recorded by John Strype from St Alfege's Church in Greenwich, in his continuation of John Stow's A *Survey of London*, published in 1720. It was said to be in the chancel and inscribed in old letters on a brass plate embedded in a stone before the altar rails:

Enterred here doth ly a worthy Wyght
Who for long Tyme in Musick bore the Bell:
His Name to shew, was Thomas Tallys hyght,
In honest vertuous Lyff he dyd excell.

He serv'd long Tyme in Chappel with grete prayse,
Fower Sovereygnes Reygnes (a Thing not often seen)
I mean Kyng Henry and Prynce Edward's Dayes,
Quene Mary, and Elizabeth our Quene.

He maryed was, though Children he had none,
And lyv'd in Love full thre and thirty Yeres,
Wyth loyal Spowse, whos Name yclyipt was Jone,
Who here entomb'd, him Company now bears.

As he did lyve, so also did he dy,
In myld and quyet Sort (O! happy Man)
To God ful oft for Mercy did he cry,
Wherefore he lyves, let Death do what he can.

Sidney Sussex College, Cambridge

Sources

A partial list of primary sources dating from before the Commonwealth is provided below. For the anthems and Dorian Evening Service, the earliest and most complete sources were consulted; the Preces and Responses are based on the version as in Barnard (1641), while the Psalter is drawn from Archbishop Parker's own annotated edition now in Corpus Christi College Library, Cambridge.

For further information including a full list of sources and variants, see *Thomas Tallis: English Sacred Music*, vols 1 and 2, Early English Church Music, 12 and 13, ed. Leonard Ellinwood, rev. Paul Doe (London: Stainer & Bell, 1971/73).

The Tallis Psalter

Matthew Parker, *The whole Psalter translated into English Metre, which contayneth an hundreth and fifty Psalmes* (London: John Day, 1567). Consulted copy: Parker Library, Corpus Christi College, Cambridge, SP.1. This contains annotations in Matthew Parker's own hand, but none are relevant to the psalms set by Tallis.

Dorian Evening Service: Magnificat & Nunc dimittis

Cambridge, Peterhouse Library, MSS 35-7, 42-45 (lacking Contratenor Cantoris), from the 'latter' set of the Caroline part-books, *c.*1635.
London, Lambeth Palace Library, MS 764 (Bass Decani only), *c.* 1630.
New York, Public Library, MS Mus. Res. *MNZ (Chirk) (complete), *c.* 1620-35.
Oxford, St John's College Library, MS 180 (Bass Decani only), *c.* 1630.
John Barnard, *The First Book of Selected Church Music, consisting of Services and Anthems* (London, 1641).

A new commandment

London, British Library, Add. MS 15166 (Medius only), *c.*1570.
London, British Library, Add. MS 29289 (Contratenor only), *c.* 1629.
New York, Public Library, Drexel MSS 4180-82 (lacks Bass), *c.* 1625.

Blessed are those that be undefiled

Cambridge, King's College, Rowe Music Library, MS 316 (Treble only), *c.* 1580.
Chelmsford, Essex County Record Office, MS D/DP Z6/1 (Bass only), *c.* 1590.
London, British Library, Add. MS 22597 (Tenor only), *c.* 1590.
London, British Library, Add. MSS 29401-5 (complete), after 1613.
Oxford, Bodleian Library, MSS Tenbury 1469-71 (Treble, Mean and Bass only), *c.* 1600.
Oxford, Bodleian Library, MSS Tenbury 354-8 (complete), *c.* 1615.

Hear the voice and prayer

Oxford, Bodleian Library, MSS Mus. Sch. e 420-2 (lacking Tenor), the Wanley Manuscripts, 1546-9.
London, British Library, Add. MS 29289 (Contratenor only), *c.* 1629.
New York, Public Library, Drexel MSS 4180-83 (complete), *c.* 1625.
New York, Public Library, MS Mus. Res. *MNZ (Chirk) (complete), *c.* 1620-35.
John Day, *Certain Notes Set forthe in foure and three partes* (London, 1565) (complete).

If ye love me
Oxford, Bodleian Library, MSS Mus. Sch. e 420-2 (lacking Tenor), the 'Wanley' manuscripts, 1546-9.
London, British Library, Add. MS 15166 (Medius only), *c.* 1570.
New York, Public Library, Drexel MSS 4180-83 (complete), *c.* 1625.
New York, Public Library, MS Mus. Res. *MNZ (Chirk) (complete), *c.* 1620-35.
John Day, *Certain Notes Set forthe in foure and three partes* (London, 1560).

O Lord, give thy Holy Spirit
London, British Library, Add. MS 15166 (Medius only), *c.* 1570.
London, British Library, Add. MS 29289 (Contratenor only), *c.* 1629.
New York, Public Library, Drexel MSS 4180-83 (complete), *c.* 1625.
John Barnard, *The First Book of Selected Church Music, consisting of Services and Anthems* (London, 1641).

O Lord, in thee is all my trust
New York, Public Library, MS Mus. Res. *MNZ (Chirk) (complete), *c.* 1620-35.
John Day, *Certain Notes Set forthe in foure and three partes* (London, 1565) (complete).

Out from the deep
Oxford, Christ Church Library, MS 6 (organ book), *c.* 1630.
New York, Public Library, MS Mus. Res. *MNZ (Chirk) (complete), *c.* 1620-35.

Purge me, O Lord
London, British Library, Add. MS 30515, Mulliner's organ book, 1545-1570.
London, British Library, Add. MS 30480-83 (complete), before 1615.

Remember not, O Lord God
London, British Library, Royal App. MSS 74-76 (lacking Bass), *c.* 1547. An early, unembellished, version; Day, below, is followed for this edition.
London, British Library, Add. MS 30515, Mulliner's organ book, 1545-1570.
London, British Library, Add. MS 29289 (Contratenor only), *c.* 1629.
John Day, *Certain Notes Set forthe in foure and three partes* (London, 1565) (complete).

Verily, verily, I say unto you
Cambridge, Peterhouse Library, MSS 34, 38, 39 (lacking Tenor), from the 'former' set of the Caroline part-books, *c.* 1635.
London, British Library, Add. MS 15166 (Medius only), *c.* 1570.

The Tallis Psalter
Psalms and Anthems
Canticles, Preces and Responses

Nine Tunes for Archbishop Parker's Psalter

The First Tune (Psalm 1)

The first is meeke: deuout to see

MATTHEW PARKER

THOMAS TALLIS
Edited by David Skinner

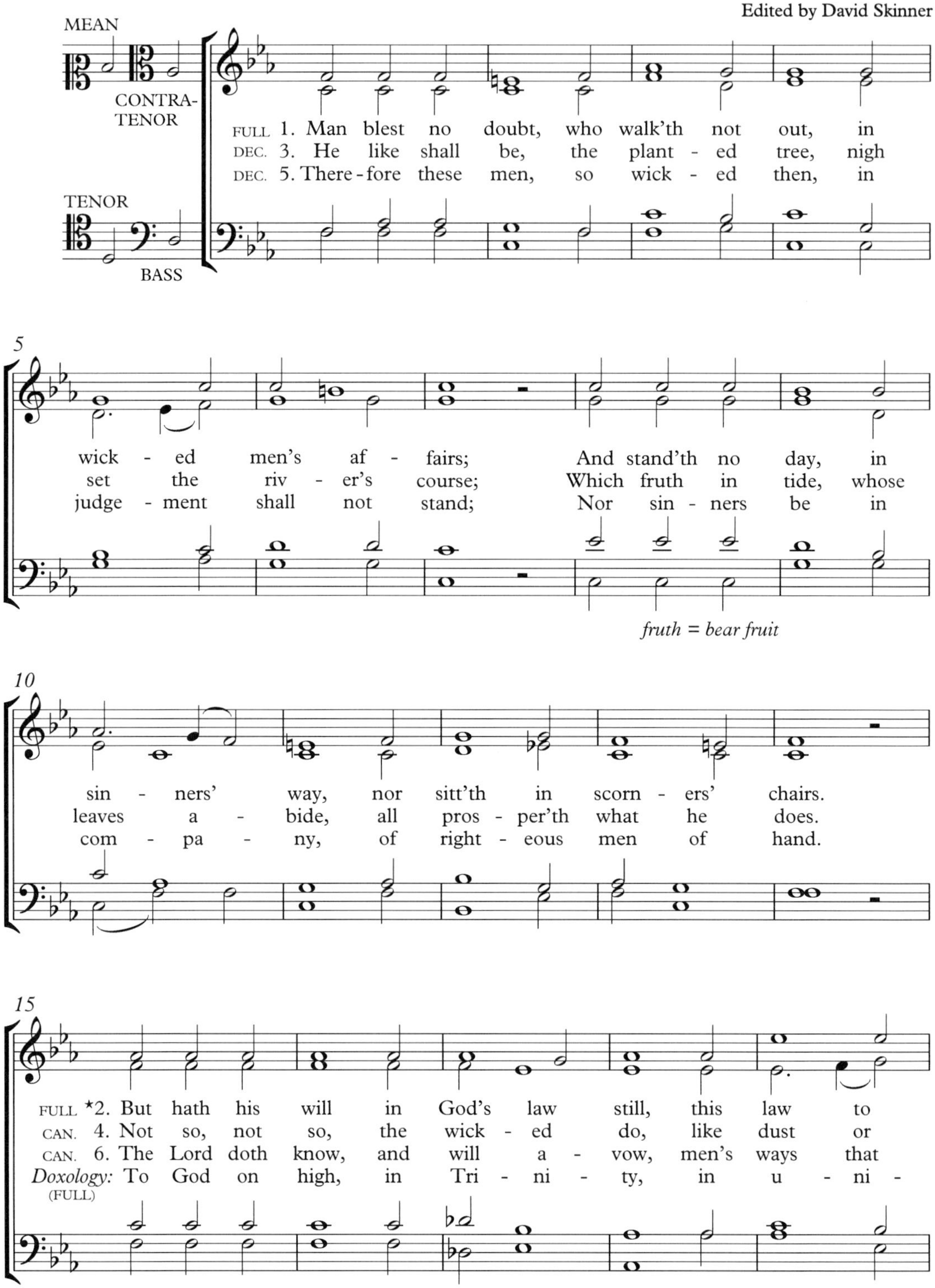

MEAN
CONTRA-TENOR
TENOR
BASS

FULL 1. Man blest no doubt, who walk'th not out, in
DEC. 3. He like shall be, the plant - ed tree, nigh
DEC. 5. There - fore these men, so wick - ed then, in

wick - ed men's af - fairs; And stand'th no day, in
set the riv - er's course; Which fruth in tide, whose
judge - ment shall not stand; Nor sin - ners be in

fruth = bear fruit

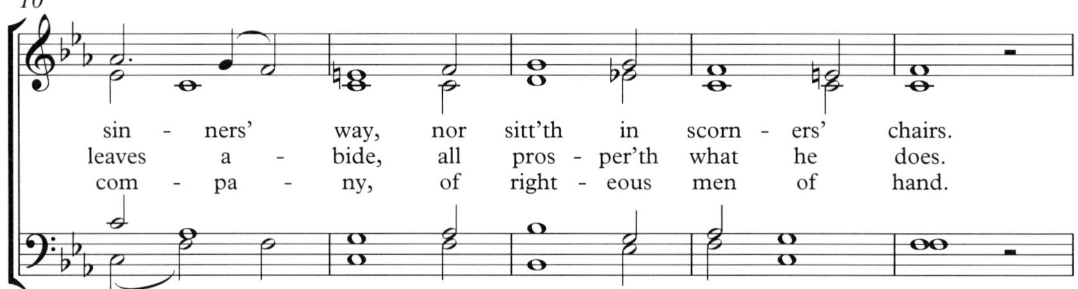

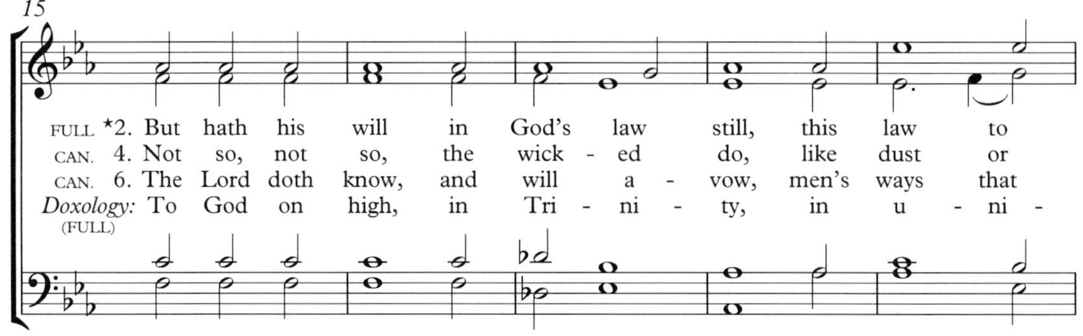

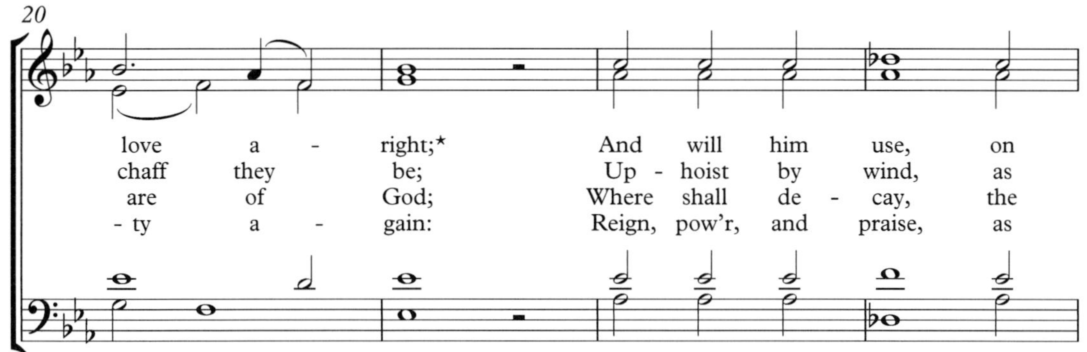

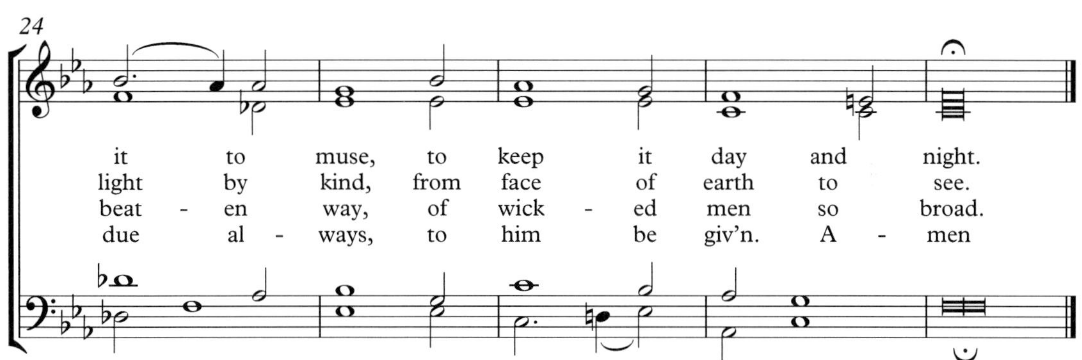

*Parker: 'But holdth euen still : God's lawe in will, with all his hartes delight.'
Tallis's version is retained here.

The Second Tune (Psalm 68)

The second is sad: in maiesty

MATTHEW PARKER

THOMAS TALLIS
Edited by David Skinner

sad = grave/firm

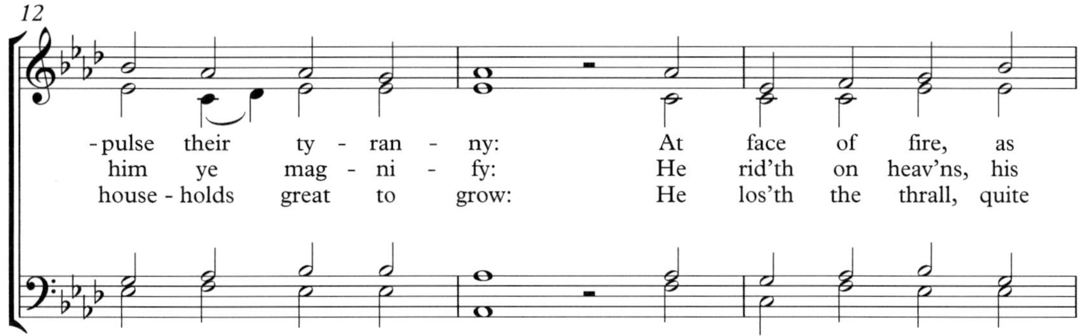

DEC. 7. O God when thou wentst forth as guide, before the people out:
When thou didst walk in wilderness, which thing thou didst no doubt,

CAN. 8. The earth then shook at face of God, the heav'ns did drop and swell:
Mount Sinaï, God's face did fear, God's face of Israël.

DEC. 9. Thou pourd'st, O God, thy fruitful showers, on thine inheritance,
When faint they were, with ease again, their strength thou didst advance.

CAN. 10. Thy church and flock to dwell therein, thou shalt it thus refresh:
So thou prepard'st for all thy poor, O God, in gentleness.

DEC. 11. Such good effect, God gave his word, to them he shewed his might:
They did outpreach his armies strong, how they excelled in fight.

CAN. 12. Now kings with hosts most fiercely set, yet fled discomfited:
And households whole, that kept at home, the spoil they did divide.

DEC. 13. Though ye have lain among the pots, as black as coal in sight:
Ye shall be white, as dove with wings, milk white and feathers bright.

CAN. 14. When God great kings threw out of land, though earst his flock was black,
Then 'gan they look as white as snow as lieth on salmon's back.

DEC. 15. God's hill is fat, as Bashan hill, a mount that stately standth:
With cliffs on high, like Bashan mount, it ris'th, it is so grand.

CAN. 16. Why leap ye so, to spite this mount, ye toppy hillocks gay:
This is God's mount where God hath dwelt, he there shall dwell for aye.

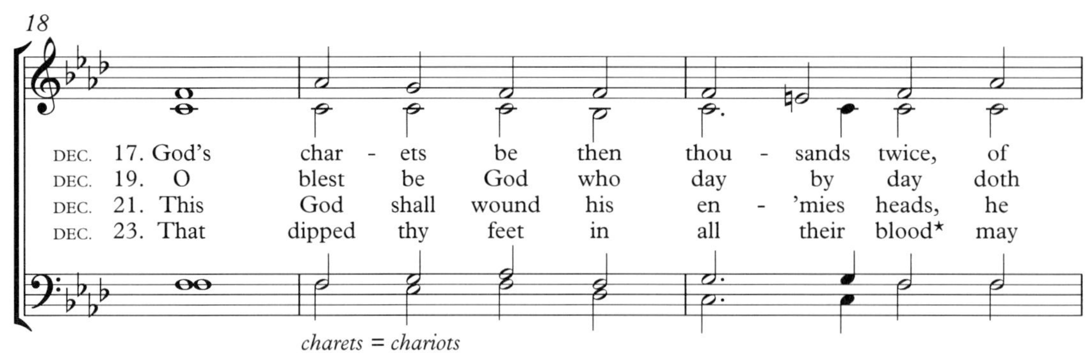
18
DEC. 17. God's char - ets be then thou - sands twice, of
DEC. 19. O blest be God who day by day doth
DEC. 21. This God shall wound his en - 'mies heads, he
DEC. 23. That dipped thy feet in all their blood* may
charets = chariots

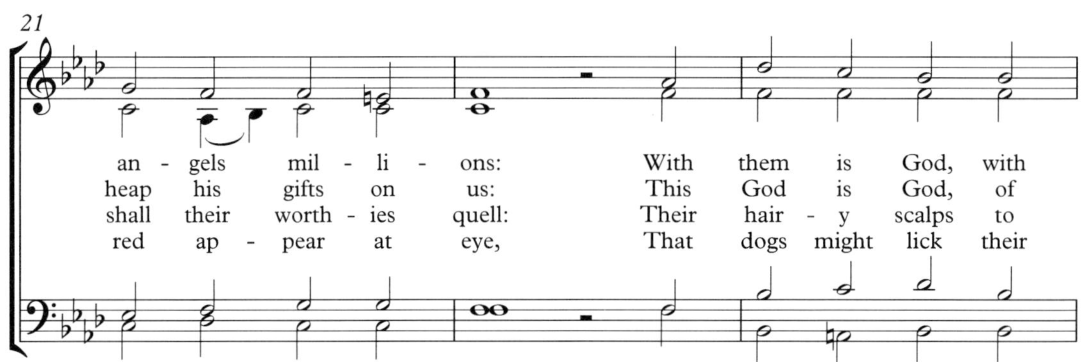
21
an - gels mil - li - ons: With them is God, with
heap his gifts on us: This God is God, of
shall their worth - ies quell: Their hair - y scalps to
red ap - pear at eye, That dogs might lick their

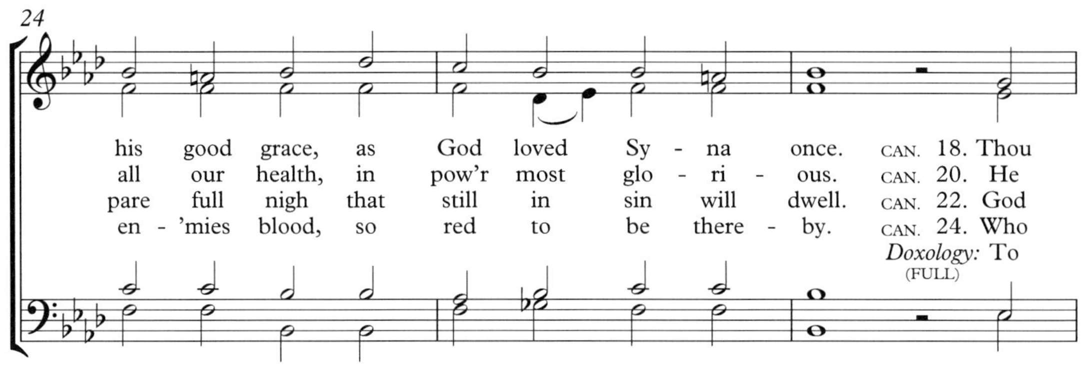
24
his good grace, as God loved Sy - na once. CAN. 18. Thou
all our health, in pow'r most glo - ri - ous. CAN. 20. He
pare full nigh that still in sin will dwell. CAN. 22. God
en - 'mies blood, so red to be there - by. CAN. 24. Who
Doxology: To
(FULL)

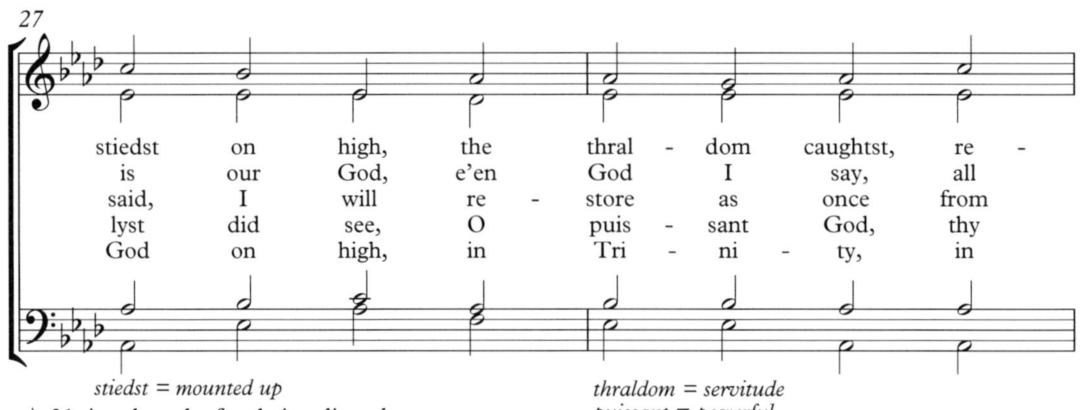
27
stiedst on high, the thral - dom caughtst, re -
is our God, e'en God I say, all
said, I will re - store as once from
lyst did see, O puis - sant God, thy
God on high, in Tri - ni - ty, in
stiedst = mounted up
thraldom = servitude
puissant = powerful
*v21: i.e. that, thy feet being dipped

DEC. 25. When thanks were sung, first singers went, then minstrels moved their feet:
In mids[t] were set the damsel maids who played with timbrels sweet.

CAN. 26. When they in one were jointly met, thus God they praisèd well:
From heart the ground they blessed the Lord, who sprang of Israël.

DEC. 27. Small Benjamin, their ruler went, so Judas tribe their stone:
So went the peers of Zebulon and Neptaly came on.

CAN. 28. Thus God hath bid all strength and power for thee full nigh to be:
With strength, O God, confirm this work that ye hast wrought so free.

DEC. 29. From thy sweet house, Jerusalem, make this thy strength proceed:
Then kings shall bring their offerings to thee to praise thy deed.

CAN. 30. The launce men's routes once scattered wide, the people's calfs once tamed:
When they shall stoop and presents bring and warring folks once shamed,

DEC. 31. Then shall the peers of Egypt land, for this come meek in sight:
Then Ethiops full soon shall yield to God their hands and might.

CAN. 32. O all ye realms of all the earth, sing ye to God of bliss:
Sing psalms and hymns to testify how worthy praise he is.

DEC. 33. To him that rid'th on heaven of heavens, as he hath done of old:
Lo he his voice hath uttered forth, a voice most strong and bold.

CAN. 34. Ascribe to God all strength and might, to Israël so showed:
On whom his power no less is wrought than is on heaven bestowed.

FULL 35. **[Second part]** O God thou art full terrible from out thy sanctuary:
This Jacob's God, his people aid'th, O blest be God thereby.

Doxology (FULL)

v.30 launce = lance

The Third Tune (Psalm 2)

The third doth rage: and roughly brayth

MATTHEW PARKER

THOMAS TALLIS
Edited by David Skinner

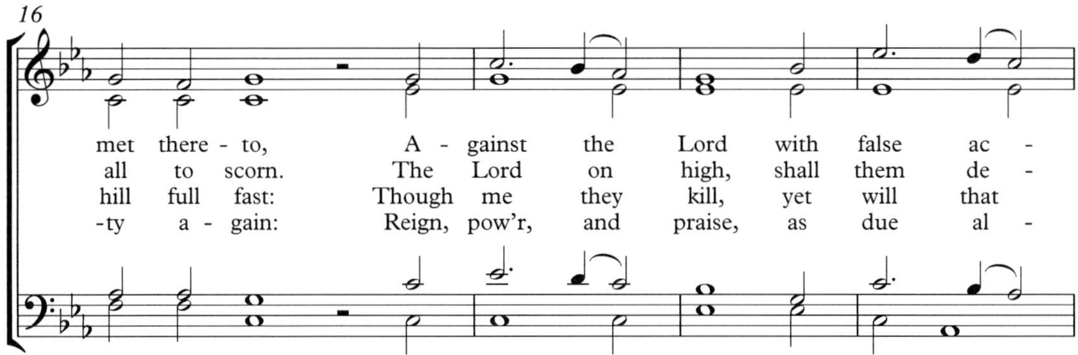

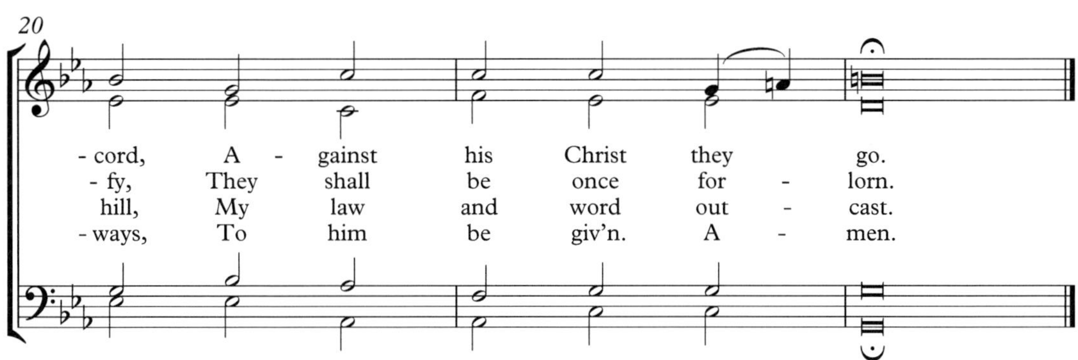

DEC. 7. God's words decreed, I, Christ, will spread
For God thus said to me:
My Son I say, thou art this day,
I have begotten thee.

CAN. 8. Ask thou of me, I will give thee,
To rule all Gentiles' lands:
Thou shalt possess, in sureness
The world how wide it stands.

DEC. 9. With iron rod, as mighty God,
All rebels shalt thou bruise:
And break them all, in pieces small,
As shards the potters use.

CAN. 10. Be wise therefore, ye kings the more,
Receive ye wisdom's lore:
The judges strong, of right and wrong,
Advise you now before.

DEC. 11. The Lord in fear, your service bear,
With dread to him rejoice:
Let rages be, resist not ye,
Him serve with joyful voice.

CAN. 12. The Son kiss ye, lest wroth he be,
Lose not the way of rest:
For when his ire is set on fire,
Who trust in him be blest.

Doxology. (FULL)

The Fourth Tune (Psalm 95)

The fourth doth fawne: and flattry playth

* 'health'; Parker's original reading is used here.

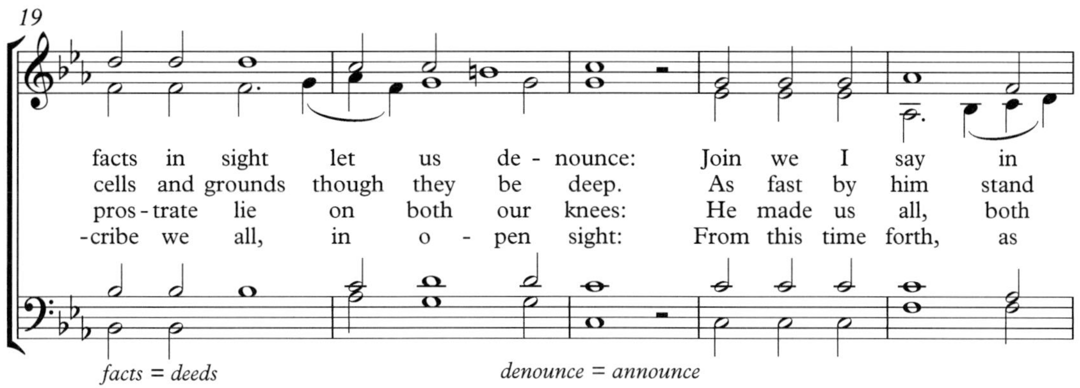

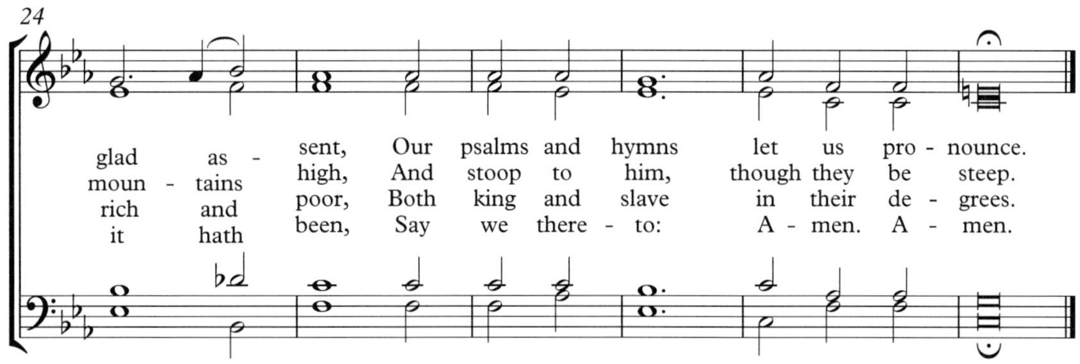

DEC. 7. For God he is, our Lord and stay,
His people we in pasture near:
His flock of hand, who lead'th our way,
His voice today if well ye hear.

CAN. 8. Beware, say I, ye hard no hearts
Against his grace to you so meant:
As desert saw, once strife o'erthwart,
Like tempting day of mad intent.

DEC. 9. In which pastime, your fathers old,
Did tempt my strength to prove my might:
They proved but me, in scorn too bold,
Where yet my works they saw in sight.

CAN. 10. Full forty years, I blamed this age;
Great griefs by them, I felt by this:
I said ev'n thus, to spy their rage,
They err in heart, my ways they miss.

FULL 11. **[2nd part]** To whom I sware, all wrathfully,
By their foul strays, thus forced thereto:
If they so ev'l my rest should see,
Then blame have I, if it be so.

Doxology. (FULL)

v.8: o'erthwart = overthurned

The Fifth Tune (Psalm 42)

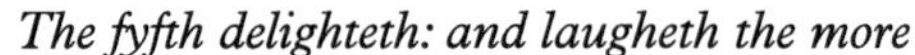

The fyfth delighteth: and laugheth the more

MATTHEW PARKER

THOMAS TALLIS
Edited by David Skinner

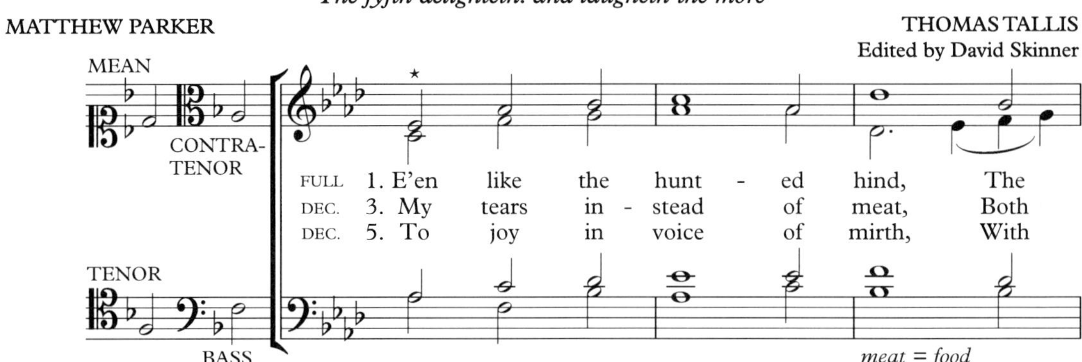

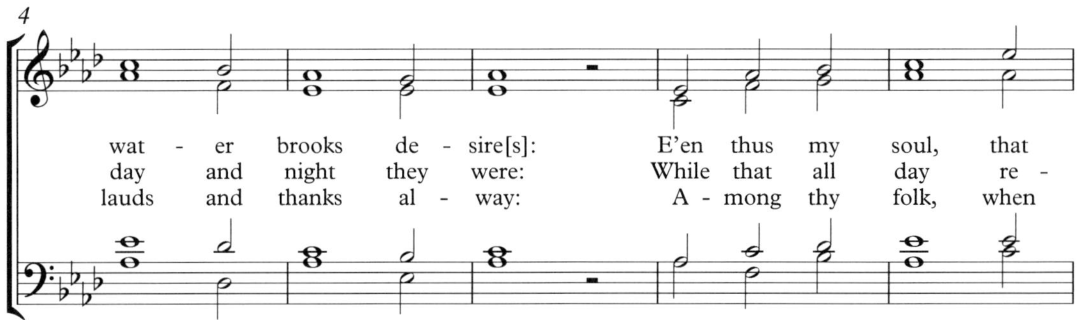

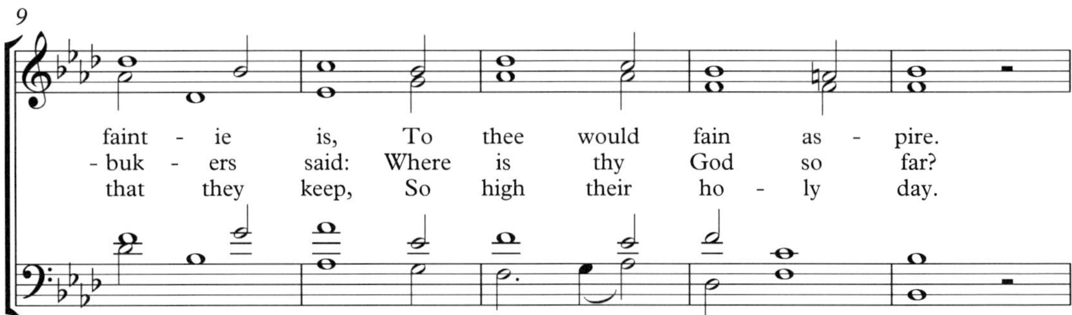

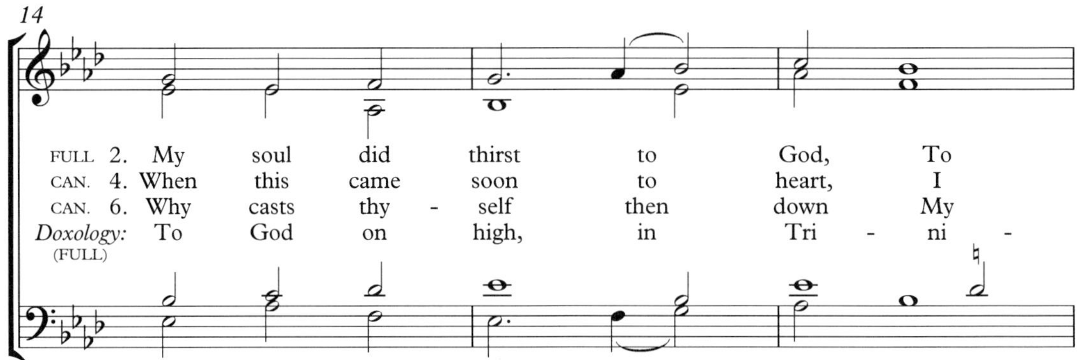

* Mean first note notated a tone higher in the source, creating a first inversion chord; this has been changed to conform with the repeated phrase in b.7.

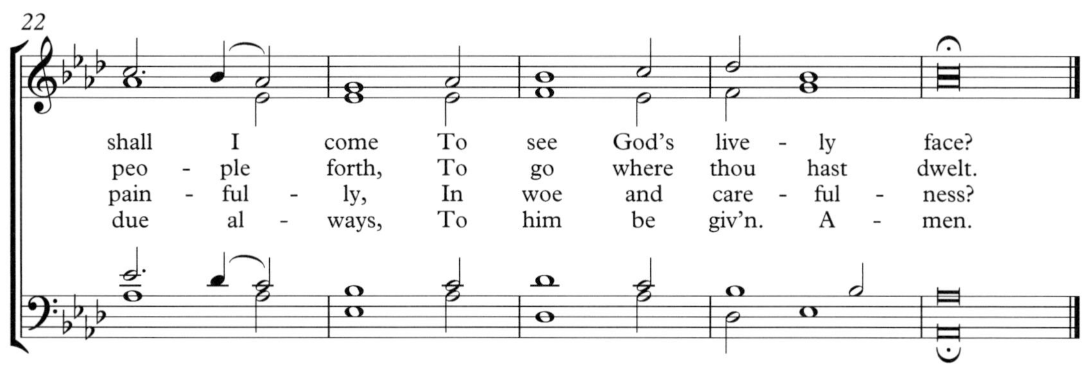

DEC. 7. Put thou thy trust in God,
Let thing[s] not thee amaze:
I will him thank for all his help,
In sight of his good grace.

CAN. 8. My God, my soul is vexed
With inward pains so thrill:
I mind thy works, in Jordan yet,
So done next Hermon hill.

DEC. 9. As deep to deep rebound'th
At noise of thy great show'rs;
Thy streams by course so overflows,
My soul the paid devours.

CAN. 10. But God yet will, the day
To shine, me grace to see:
My night of woe shall praise him then,
Who kept yet life in me.

DEC. 11. Thou are my strength, O God,
I might then plain in woe:
Why hast me thus forgot so quite,
So sad to go for foe?

CAN. 12. It pierc'th my bones as sword
To hear my foes in spite:
They daily thus at me upbraid:
Where is thy God of might?

DEC. 13. Why art thou then, my soul
So vexed and prostrate so:
Why mak'st in me so much ado,
Where God is friend in woe?

CAN. 14. O put thy hope in God,
I trust in time and place:
He is my God, whom I will thank,
My face shall see his grace.

Doxology. (FULL)

v12: upbraid = reproach

The Sixth Tune (Psalm 5)

The sixt bewayleth: it weepeth full sore

MATTHEW PARKER

THOMAS TALLIS
Edited by David Skinner

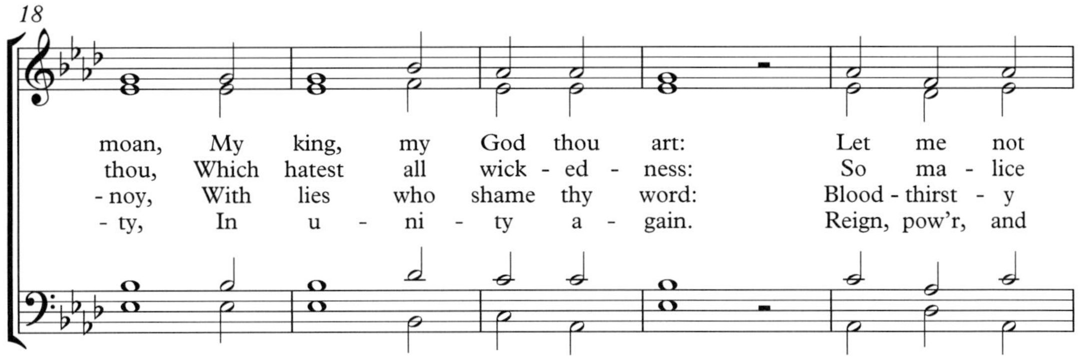

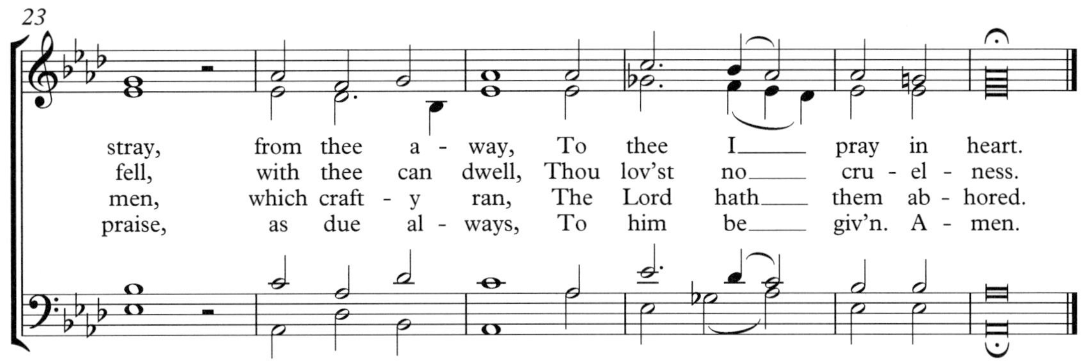

DEC. 7. Just will I go, thy house into,
In trust of thy great grace:
In fear I will do honour still,
Against that holy place.

CAN. 8. O Lord be guide, defend my side,
In thy great righteousness:
Make plain the way, less I do stray,
My foes shall brag the less.

DEC. 9. Their mouths express no faithfulness,
Their hollow hearts be vain:
Wide throat they have, as open grave,
Their tongue but lies do fain.

CAN. 10. Destroy their thought, O God for nought,
Their own ways be their shame:
Expell them out, in lies so stout,
Who thus blaspheme thy name.

DEC. 11. Let them rejoice, that trust thy voice,
Aye thanks they shall extend:
Who love thy name, shall joy the same,
Thou dost to them defend.

CAN. 12. Thou Lord wilt then give rightwise men,
The heav'nly bliss from thence:
Thy favour kind, is not behind
As them with shield to fence.

Doxology. (FULL)

The Seventh Tune (Psalm 52)

The seuenth tredeth stoute: in froward race

MATTHEW PARKER

THOMAS TALLIS
Edited by David Skinner

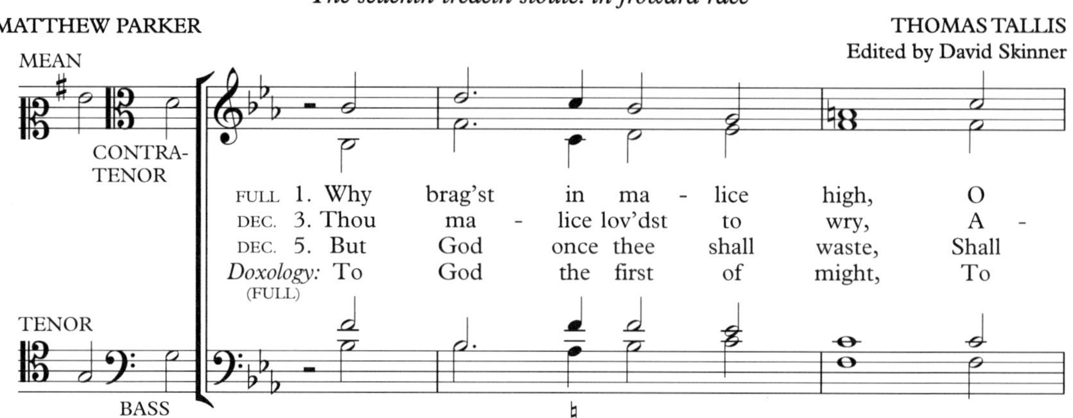

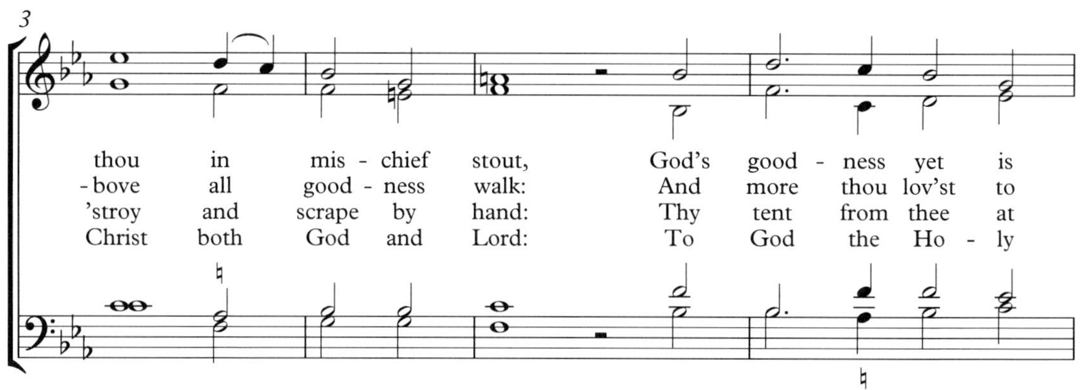

The Contra-tenor and Tenor parts have been swapped for the odd verses.

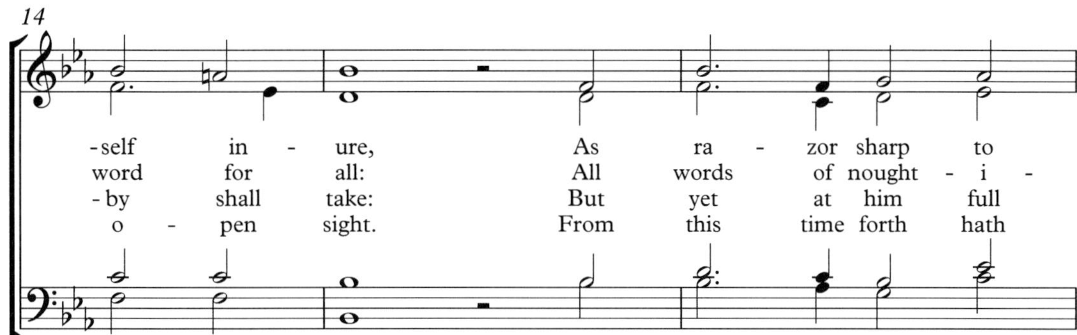

DEC. 7. O lo, the man himself,
That made not God his aid:
That trust'd in riches wealth,
Whose might in mischief laid.

CAN. 8. But I as olive green,
In God's sweet house shall lay;
My trust hath ever been,
In God's good grace for aye.

FULL 9. **[2nd part]** I thee shall laud e'en still,
For this thou didst say I:
Thy name to wait I will,
For good thy saints it spy.

Doxology. (FULL)

The Eighth Tune (Psalm 67)

The eyghte goeth milde: in modest pace

MATTHEW PARKER

THOMAS TALLIS
Edited by David Skinner

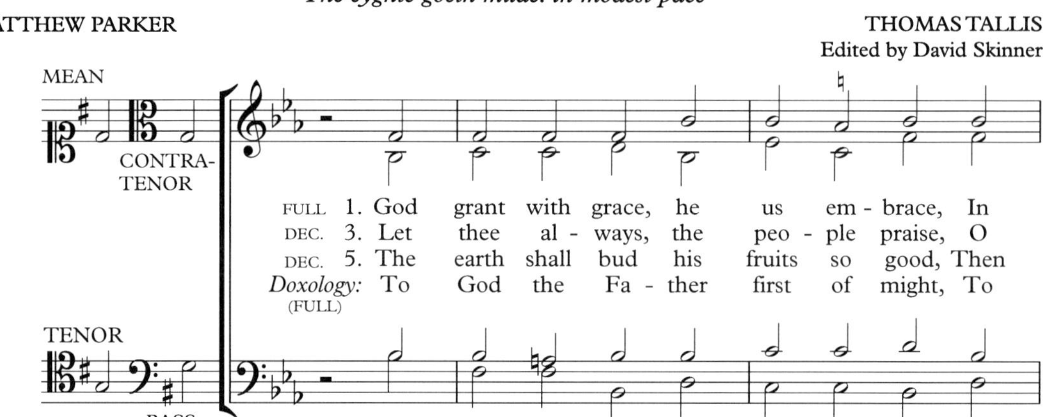

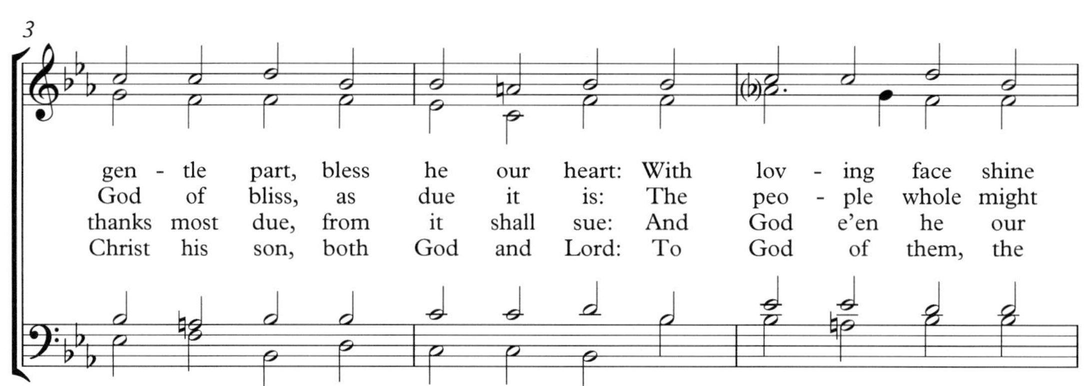

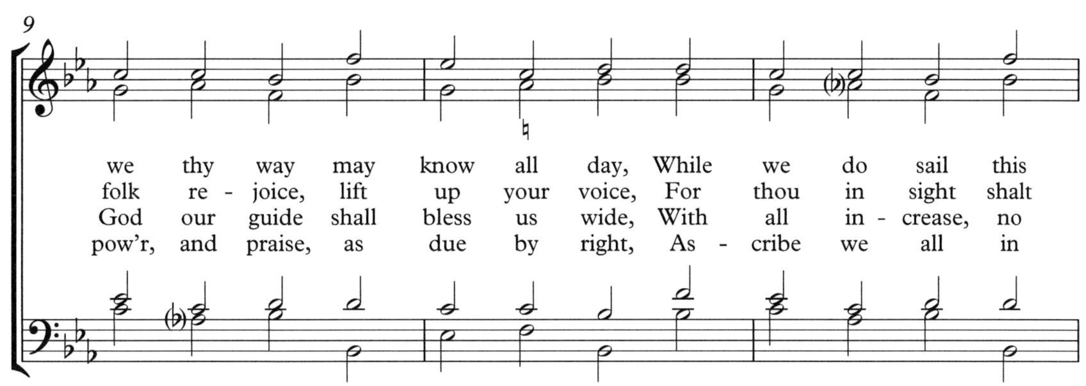
9
we thy way may know all day, While we do sail this
folk re - joice, lift up your voice, For thou in sight shalt
God our guide shall bless us wide, With all in - crease, no
pow'r, and praise, as due by right, As - cribe we all in

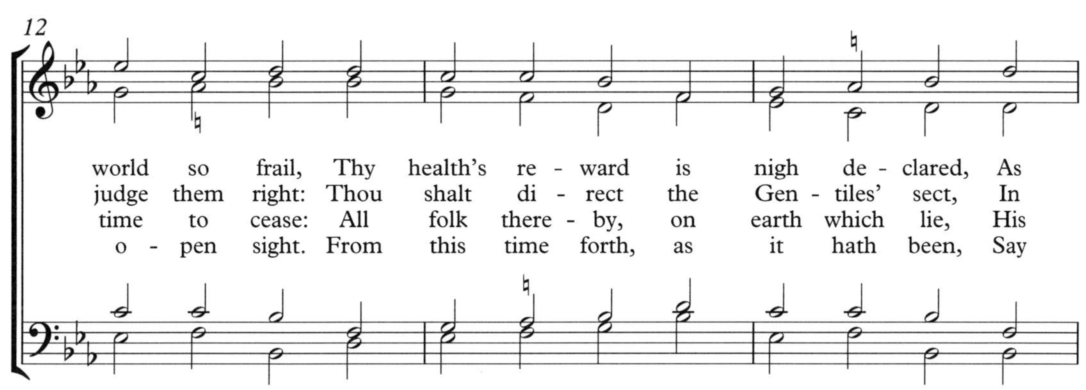
12
world so frail, Thy health's re - ward is nigh de - clared, As
judge them right: Thou shalt di - rect the Gen - tiles' sect, In
time to cease: All folk there - by, on earth which lie, His
o - pen sight. From this time forth, as it hath been, Say

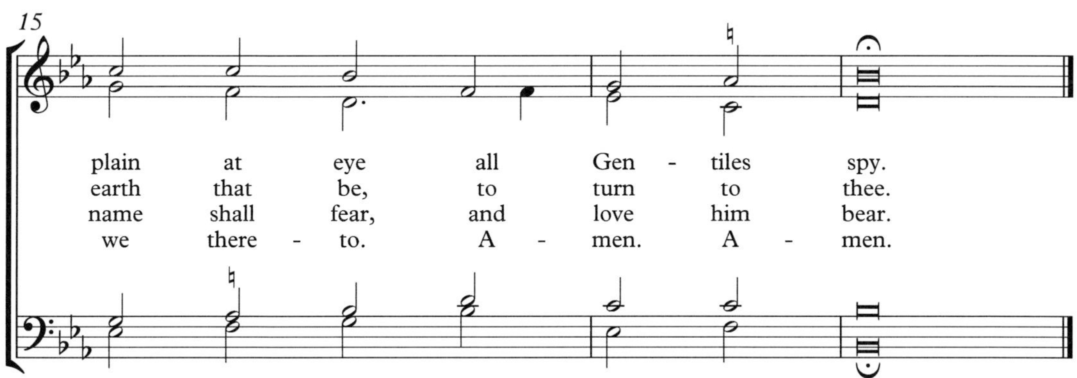
15
plain at eye all Gen - tiles spy.
earth that be, to turn to thee.
name shall fear, and love him bear.
we there - to. A - men. A - men.

Veni Creator ('Ordinal')

MATTHEW PARKER

THOMAS TALLIS
Edited by David Skinner

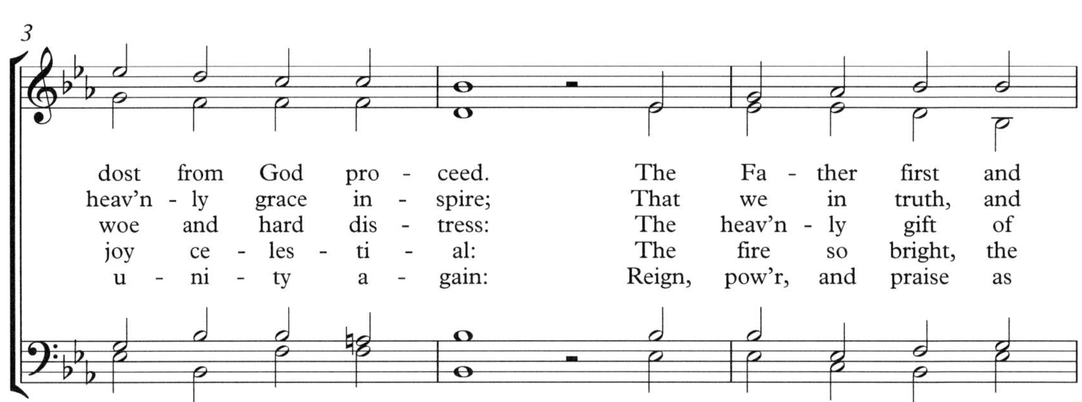

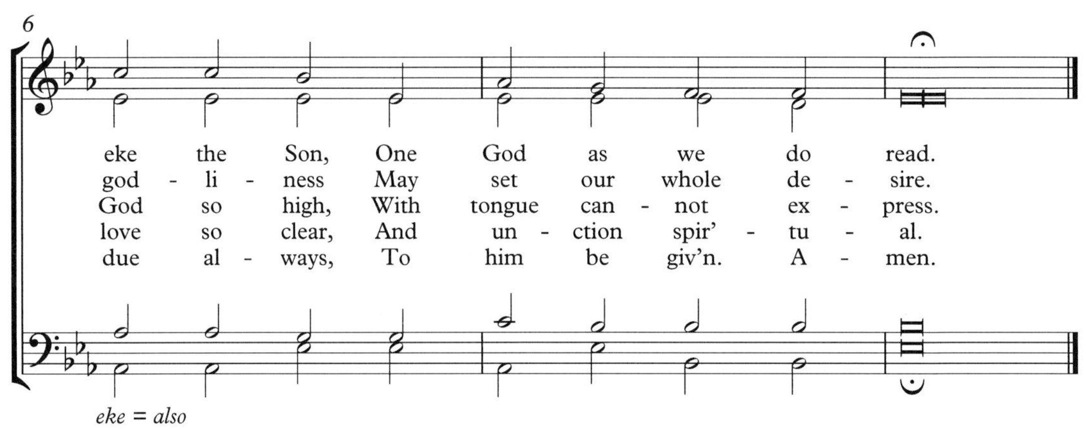

eke = *also*

CAN. 5. For thou in gifts art manifold,
Whereby Christ's church doth stand:
And wright'st thy love in faithful hearts,
The power of God his hand.

DEC. 6. And like as thou hast promise made,
Thou giv'st the speech of grace:
That through thy help, the praise of God,
May sound in every place.

CAN. 7. O Holy Ghost, to move our wits,
Send down thine heav'nly light:
Inflame our hearts, our God to serve,
With love both day and night.

DEC. 8. Our weakness strength, confirm us Lord,
Both feeble, faint and frail:
That neither flesh, the world, ne devil,
In us do once prevail.

CAN. 9. Put back from us our enemies,
And grant that we obtain
Sweet peace of heart, with God and man,
From grudge and proud disdain.

DEC. 10. And grant, O Lord, O leader sure,
That we by thee as guide
May safe eschew the snares of sin,
From thee no time to slide.

CAN. 11. And plenty Lord, of thy good grace,
Grant us we humble pray:
Be thou our joy, and comforter,
To 'scape that dreadful day.

DEC. 12. Of strife and foul dissention,
O Lord dissolve the bands,
And knit the knot of peace and love,
Throughout all Christian lands.

CAN. 13. Grant us, O Lord, through thee to know,
The Father most of might,
That we of his beloved son,
May sure obtain the fight.

DEC. 14. And that with perfect stable saith,
We might acknowledge thee:
The sprite of them, of both I say,
One God and persons three.

CAN. 15. Be laud to God, the father high,
And God his son praise ye:
Be praise to God, the holy sprite,
One God in Trinity.

FULL 16. Pray we that Christ the saviour
Vouchsafe his sprite to send:
To all which true profess his name,
Till all the world doth end.

Doxology. (FULL)

Preces and Responses

THOMAS TALLIS
Edited by David Skinner

As it was in the be - gin - ning, is now,
As it was in the be - gin - ning, is now,
As it was in the be - gin - ning, is now,

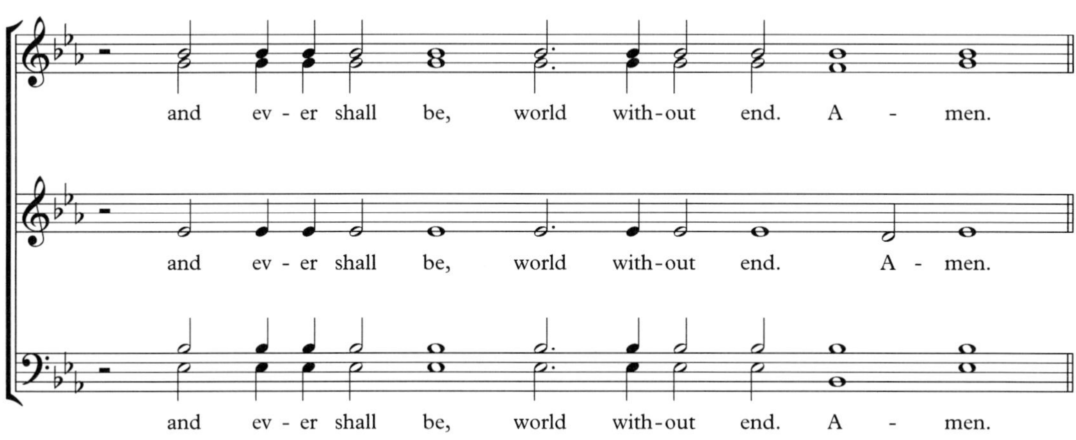
and ev - er shall be, world with-out end. A - men.
and ev - er shall be, world with-out end. A - men.
and ev - er shall be, world with-out end. A - men.

Praise ye the Lord. Praise ye the Lord.
Praise ye the Lord. Praise ye the Lord.
Praise ye the Lord. Praise ye the Lord.
Praise ye the Lord. Praise ye the Lord.

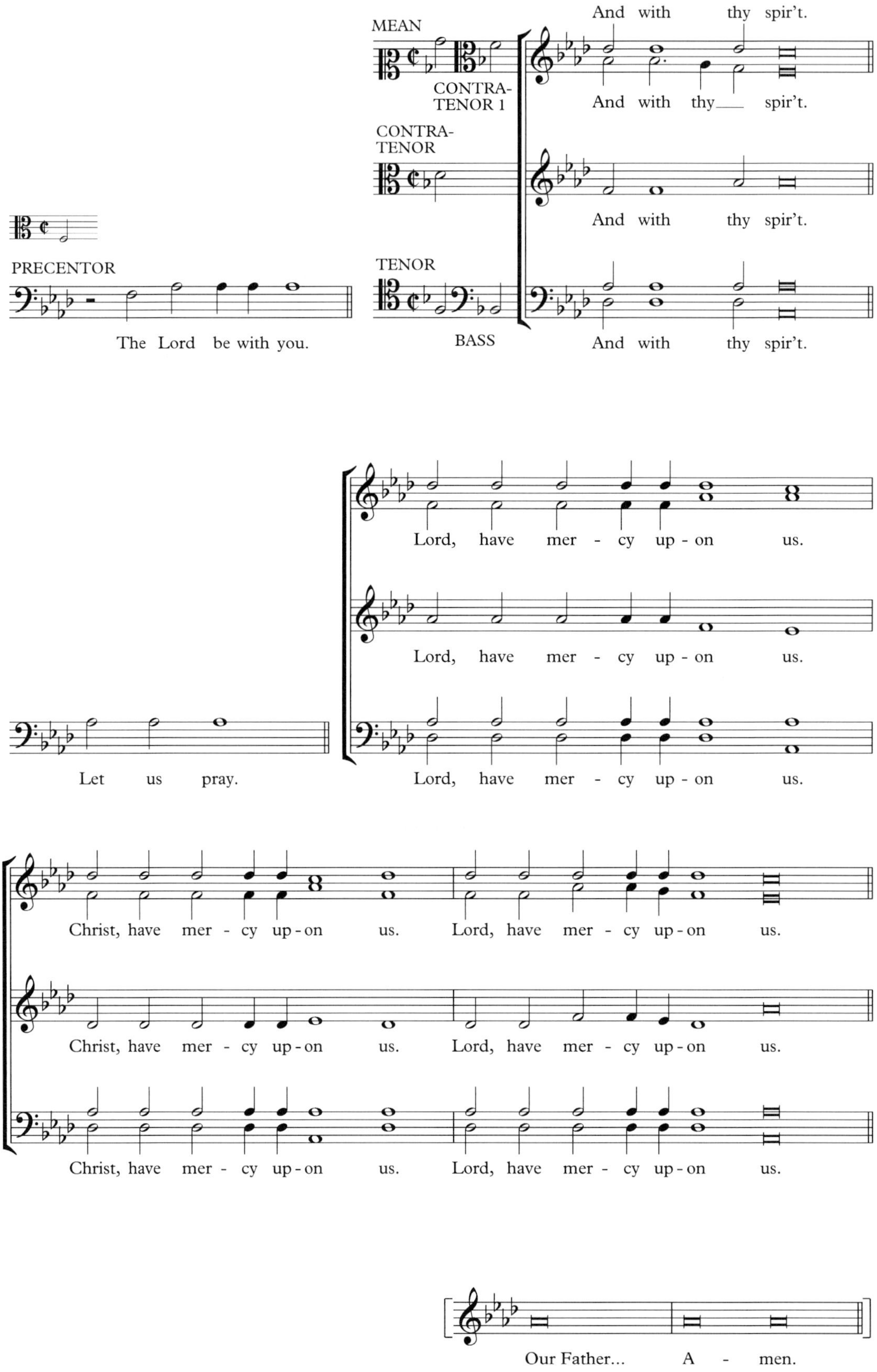
MEAN
CONTRA-TENOR 1
CONTRA-TENOR
TENOR
BASS
PRECENTOR
The Lord be with you.
And with thy spir't.
And with thy spir't.
And with thy spir't.
And with thy spir't.
Let us pray.
Lord, have mer - cy up - on us.
Lord, have mer - cy up - on us.
Lord, have mer - cy up - on us.
Christ, have mer - cy up - on us. Lord, have mer - cy up - on us.
Christ, have mer - cy up - on us. Lord, have mer - cy up - on us.
Christ, have mer - cy up - on us. Lord, have mer - cy up - on us.
Our Father... A - men.

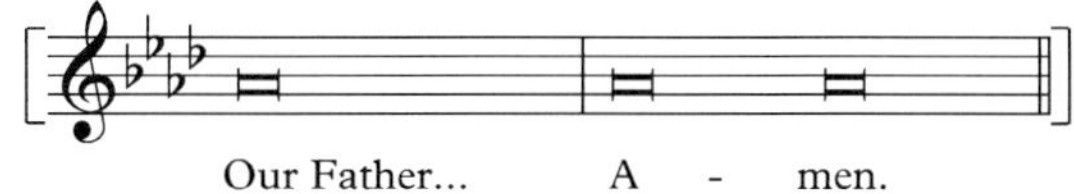

And grant us thy sal - va - ti - on.
And grant us thy sal - va - ti - on.
O Lord, shew thy mer - cy up-on us.
And grant us thy sal - va - ti - on.
And mer-ci-ful-ly hear us when we call up - on thee.
And mer-ci-ful-ly hear us when we call up - on thee.
O Lord, save the Queen.
And mer-ci-ful-ly hear us when we call up - on thee.
And make thy cho-sen peo-ple joy-ful.
And make thy cho-sen peo-ple joy - ful.
And make thy cho-sen peo-ple joy - ful.
En-due thy mi-nis-ters with right-eous-ness.
And make thy cho-sen peo-ple joy - ful.
And bless thine in-her - i-tance.
And bless thine in-her - i-tance.
O Lord, save thy peo - ple.
And bless thine in-her - i-tance.

Give peace in our time, O Lord.
Be - cause there is none oth - er
Be - cause there is none oth - er
Be - cause there is none oth - er
that fight - eth for us, but on - ly thou, O God.
that fight - eth for us, but on - ly thou, O God.
that fight - eth for us, but on - ly thou, O God.
O God, make clean our hearts with - in us.
And take not thy
And take not thy
And take not thy
Ho - ly Spi - rit from us.
Ho - ly Spi - rit from us.
Ho - ly Spi - rit from us.
A - men. A - men. A - men.
A - men. A - men. A - men.
A - men. A - men. A - men.

The Dorian Service

This setting may also be performed a minor third lower for ATBarB

-gard - ed the low - li-ness of his hand-maid-en. For be-hold from hence-
-gard - ed the low - li-ness of his hand-maid-en. For be-hold from hence -
- gard-ed the low-li-ness of his hand-maid-en. For be-hold from hence -
-gard - ed the low - li-ness of his hand-maid-en. For be-hold from hence -

-forth all ge-ne-ra - ti-ons shall call me bless - ed. For he that is
-forth all ge-ne-ra - ti - ons shall call me bless - ed. For he that is
-forth all ge - ne - ra - ti-ons shall call me bless - ed. For he that is
-forth all ge-ne-ra - ti-ons shall call me bless - ed. For he that is

20
might - y hath mag - ni-fied me; and Ho - ly is his name. And his mer -
might - y hath mag - ni-fied me; and Ho - ly is his name. And his mer -
might - y hath mag - ni-fied me; and Ho - ly is his name. And his mer -
might - y hath mag - ni-fied me; and Ho - ly is his name. And his mer -
25
- cy is on them that fear him, through-out all ge - ne - ra - ti - ons.
- cy is on them that fear him, through-out all ge - ne - ra - ti - ons.
- cy is on them that fear him, through-out all ge - ne - ra - ti - ons.
- cy is on them that fear him, through-out all ge - ne - ra - ti - ons.

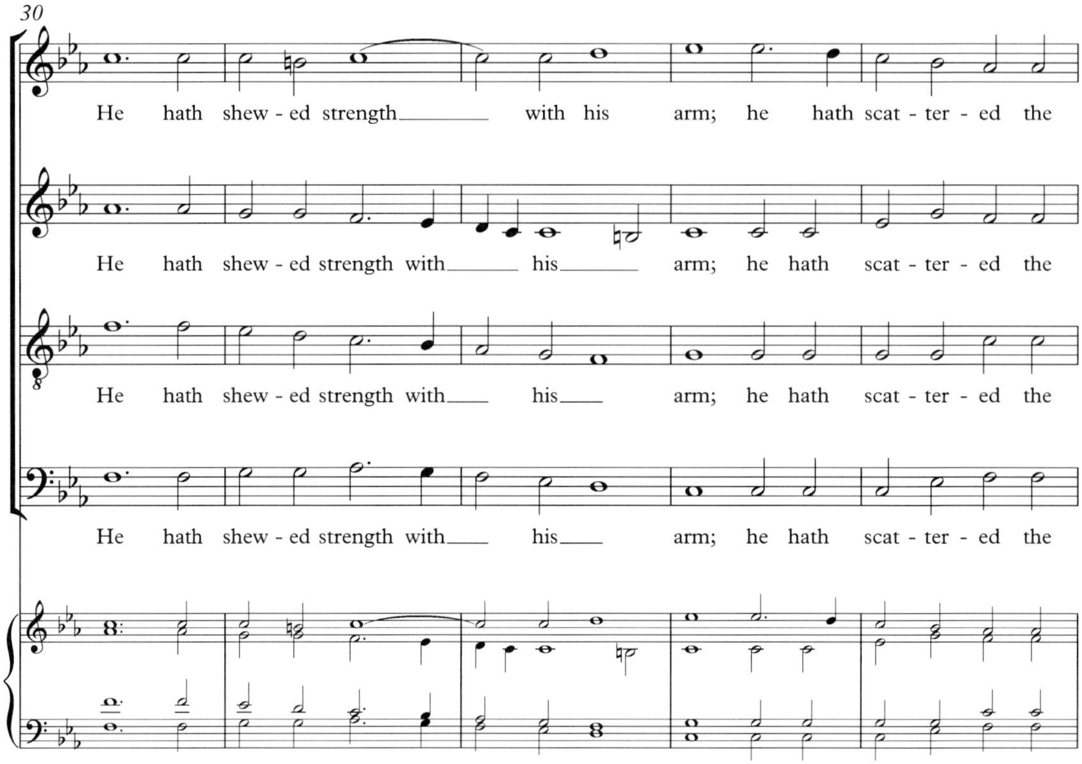
30
He hath shew - ed strength with his arm; he hath scat - ter - ed the
He hath shew - ed strength with his arm; he hath scat - ter - ed the
He hath shew - ed strength with his arm; he hath scat - ter - ed the
He hath shew - ed strength with his arm; he hath scat - ter - ed the

35
proud in the i - ma - gi - na - ti - on of their hearts.
proud in the i - ma - gi - na - ti - on of their hearts.
proud in the i - ma - gi - na - ti - on of their hearts.
proud in the i - ma - gi - na - ti - on of their hearts.

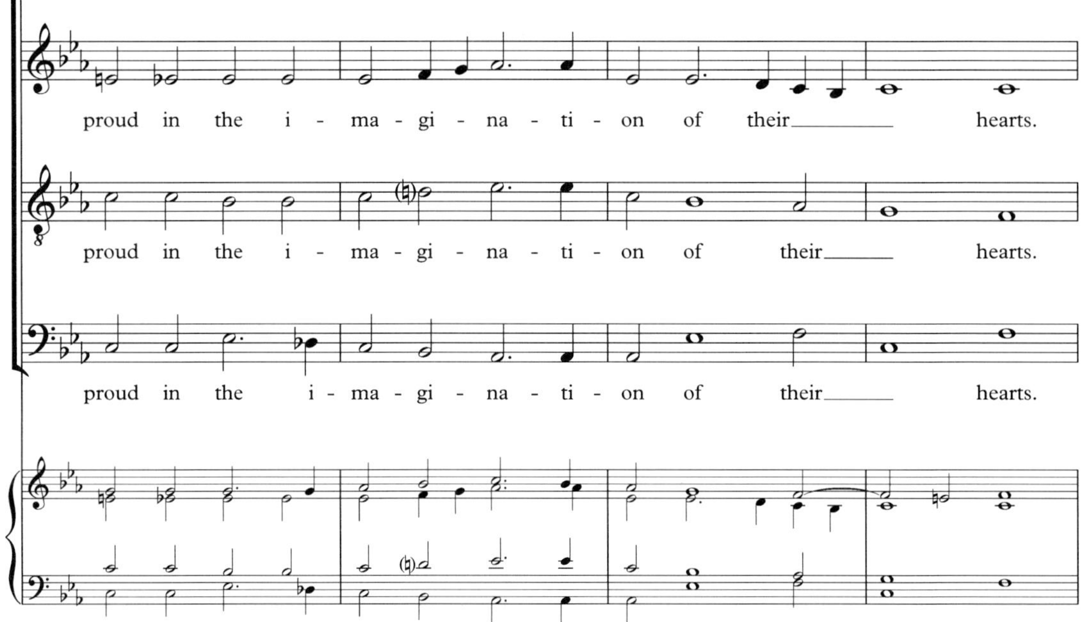

39
He hath put down the might - y from their seat, and hath ex - alt - ed
He hath put down the might - y from their seat, and hath ex - alt - ed
He hath put down the might - y from their seat, and hath ex - alt -
He hath put down the might - y from their seat, and hath ex - alt -
44
the hum - ble and meek. He hath fill - ed the
the hum - ble and meek. He hath fill - ed the
-ed the hum - ble and meek. He hath fill - ed the
-ed the hum - ble and meek. He hath fill - ed the

48
hun - gry with good things; and the rich he hath sent emp - ty a - way.
hun - gry with good things; and the rich he hath sent emp - ty a - way.
hun - gry with good things; and the rich he hath sent emp - ty a - way.
hun - gry with good things; and the rich he hath sent emp - ty a - way.
53
He re - mem - b'ring his mer - cy hath hol - pen his ser - vant Is - ra - el;
He re - mem - b'ring his mer - cy hath hol - pen his ser - vant Is - ra - el;
He re - mem - b'ring his mer - cy hath hol - pen his ser - vant Is - ra - el;
He re - mem - b'ring his mer - cy hath hol - pen his ser - vant Is - ra - el;

58

as he pro - mis-ed to our___ fore - fa - thers, A - bra-ham

as he pro - mis-ed to our___ fore-fa - thers, A - bra-ham

as he pro - mis-ed to our___ fore - fa - thers, A - bra-ham

as he pro - mis-ed to our fore - fa - thers, A - bra-ham

62

and his seed___ for ev - er. Glo - ry be to the Fa -

and his seed_____ for ev - er. Glo - ry be to the__ Fa -

and his seed for ev - er. Glo - ry be to___ the Fa -

and his seed for___ ev - er. Glo - ry be to the Fa -

66
-ther, and to the Son, and to the Ho-ly Ghost. As it was in the be-gin-
-ther, and to the Son, and to the Ho - ly Ghost. As it was in the be-gin -
-ther, and to the Son, and to the Ho - ly Ghost. As it was in the be-gin -
-ther, and to the Son, and to the Ho - ly Ghost. As it was in the be-gin -
71
- ning, is now, and ev - er shall be, world with-out end. A - men.
- ning, is now, and ev - er shall be, world with-out end. A - men.
- ning, is now, and ev - er shall be, world with-out end. A - - men.
- ning, is now, and ev - er shall be, world with-out end. A - men.

NUNC DIMITTIS

THOMAS TALLIS
Edited by David Skinner

10
sal - va - ti - on, which thou hast pre - par - ed be -
thy sal - va - ti - on, which thou hast pre - par - ed
thy sal - va - ti - on, which thou hast pre - par - ed
thy sal - va - ti - on, which thou hast pre - par - ed
14
-fore the face of all peo - ple. To be a light to light - en the
be - fore the face of all peo - ple. To be a light to light -
be - fore the face of all peo - ple. To be a light to
be - fore the face of all peo - ple. To be a light to

19
Gen - tiles, and to be the glo - ry of thy peo - ple Is - ra -
- en the Gen - tiles, and to be the glo - ry of thy peo - ple Is - ra-
light - en the Gen - tiles, and to be the glo - ry of thy peo - ple Is - ra-
light - en the Gen - tiles, and to be the glo - ry of thy peo - ple Is - ra-
23
- el. Glo - ry be to the Fa - ther, and to the Son, and
- el. Glo - ry be to the Fa - ther, and to the Son, and
- el. Glo - ry be to the Fa - ther, and to the Son, and
- el. Glo - ry be to the Fa - ther, and to the Son, and

27
to the Ho - ly Ghost. As it was in the be - gin - ning, is
to the Ho - ly Ghost. As it was in the be - gin - ning, is
to the Ho - ly Ghost. As it was in the be - gin - ning, is
to the Ho - ly Ghost. As it was in the be - gin - ning, is
31
now, and ev - er shall be, world with-out end. A - men.
now, and ev - er shall be, world with-out end. A - - - men.
now, and ev - er shall be, world with - out end. A - - men.
now, and ev - er shall be, world with - out end. A - - men.

1. A new commandment

St John, 13: 34-5

THOMAS TALLIS
Edited by David Skinner

This anthem may also be performed down a fourth for TTBarB.

8
Lord, that ye love to - geth - er, as I have
-er, that ye love to - geth - er, as I have lov - ed
- er, that ye love to-geth - - - er, as
love to - geth - er, that ye love to-geth - er, as
12
lov - ed you, as I have lov - ed you, that e'en so
you, as I have lov - ed you, as I have lov - ed you,
I have lov - ed you, lov - ed you, as I have lov - ed you, that e'en so
I have lov - ed you, as I have lov - ed you, have lov - ed you,

17
ye love one an - oth - er, that e'en so ye love one an -
that e'en so ye love one an - oth - er, an - oth - er,
ye love one an - oth - er, that e'en so ye love one
that e'en so ye love one an - oth - er, that
21
- oth - er, that e'en so ye love one an - oth - er, that
that ye love one an - oth - er, that e'en so ye love one an - oth - er,
an - oth - er, that e'en so ye love one an - oth - er, that
e'en so ye love one an - oth - er, that e'en so ye love one an - oth - er,

26
e'en so ye love one an - oth - er. By this shall ev - 'ry man
love one an - oth - er. By this shall ev - 'ry
e'en so ye love one an - oth - er. By this shall
love one an - oth - er.
30
know, ev - 'ry man know, by this shall ev - 'ry man know
man know, by this shall ev - 'ry man know that
ev - 'ry man know, by this shall ev - 'ry man
By this shall ev - 'ry man know, by this shall ev - 'ry man

34
that ye are my dis - ci - ples, that ye are my dis - ci - ples,
ye are my dis - ci-ples, that ye are my dis - ci-ples, that ye are my dis - ci -
know that ye are my dis - ci - ples, are my dis - ci - ples,
know that ye are my dis - ci-ples, that ye are my dis - ci - - ples,
39
if ye have love one to an - oth - er, if ye have love one to an -
-ples, if ye have love one to an - oth - er, to an-oth - er,
if ye have love one to an - oth - er, if ye have love one to
if ye have love one to an - oth - er, if

44
-oth - er, if ye have love one to an - oth - er, if
if ye have love one to an - oth-er, if ye have love one to an - oth - er,
an - oth - - - er, if ye have love one to an - oth - er, if
ye have love one to an - oth - er, if ye have love one to an - oth - er,
49
ye have love one to an - oth - er, love one to an - oth - er.
one to an - oth - - er, love one to an-oth - er.
ye have love one to an - oth - er, love one to an-oth - er.
one to an - oth - er, love one to an-oth - er.

2. Blessed be those that be undefiled

Psalm 119: 1-6

THOMAS TALLIS
Edited by David Skinner

9

Bless - ed are they that keep his test - i-mon -

Lord. Bless - ed are they___ that keep his test-i-mon -

Lord. Bless - ed are they that

13

-ies: and seek him with_ their_ whole___ heart, with their whole_

-ies, that keep his test - i-mon - ies: and seek him with their_

keep his test - i - mon - ies: and seek him with_ their_

17
heart.
whole heart.
whole heart.
Bless - ed are they that keep his test -
Bless - ed are they that keep his test - i - mon -
Bless - ed are they that keep his test - i -
21
- i - mon - ies: and seek him with their whole
- ies: and seek him with their whole
-mon - ies: and seek him with their whole heart, with their whole

25

For they who do no wick - ed-ness,

For they who do no wick - ed - ness, wick - ed -

heart. For they who do no wick -

heart. For they who do no

heart.

29

for they who do no wick - ed - ness:

- ness, for they who do no wick - ed - ness,

- ed - ness, who do no wick - ed - ness, for they who do no

wick - ed - ness, do no wick - ed - ness, for

For they who do no wick - ed - ness,

33

walk in his ways.

who do no wick - ed - ness: walk in his ways.

wick - ed - ness: walk in his ways.

they who do no wick - ed - ness: walk in his ways.

for they who do no wick - ed - ness: walk in his ways.

37

Thou hast charg - ed us, O Lord, that

Thou hast charg - ed us, O Lord, that

Thou hast charg - ed us, O Lord, that

41

we shall di - li - gent - ly keep thy com - mand - e - ments.

we shall di - li - gent - ly keep thy com - mand - e - ments.

we shall di - li - gent - ly keep thy com - mand - ments, thou

Thou

Thou

45

hast charg - ed us, O Lord, that we shall di - li -

hast charg - ed us, O Lord, that we shall di - li - gent - ly

hast charg - ed us, O Lord, that we shall di - li - gent -

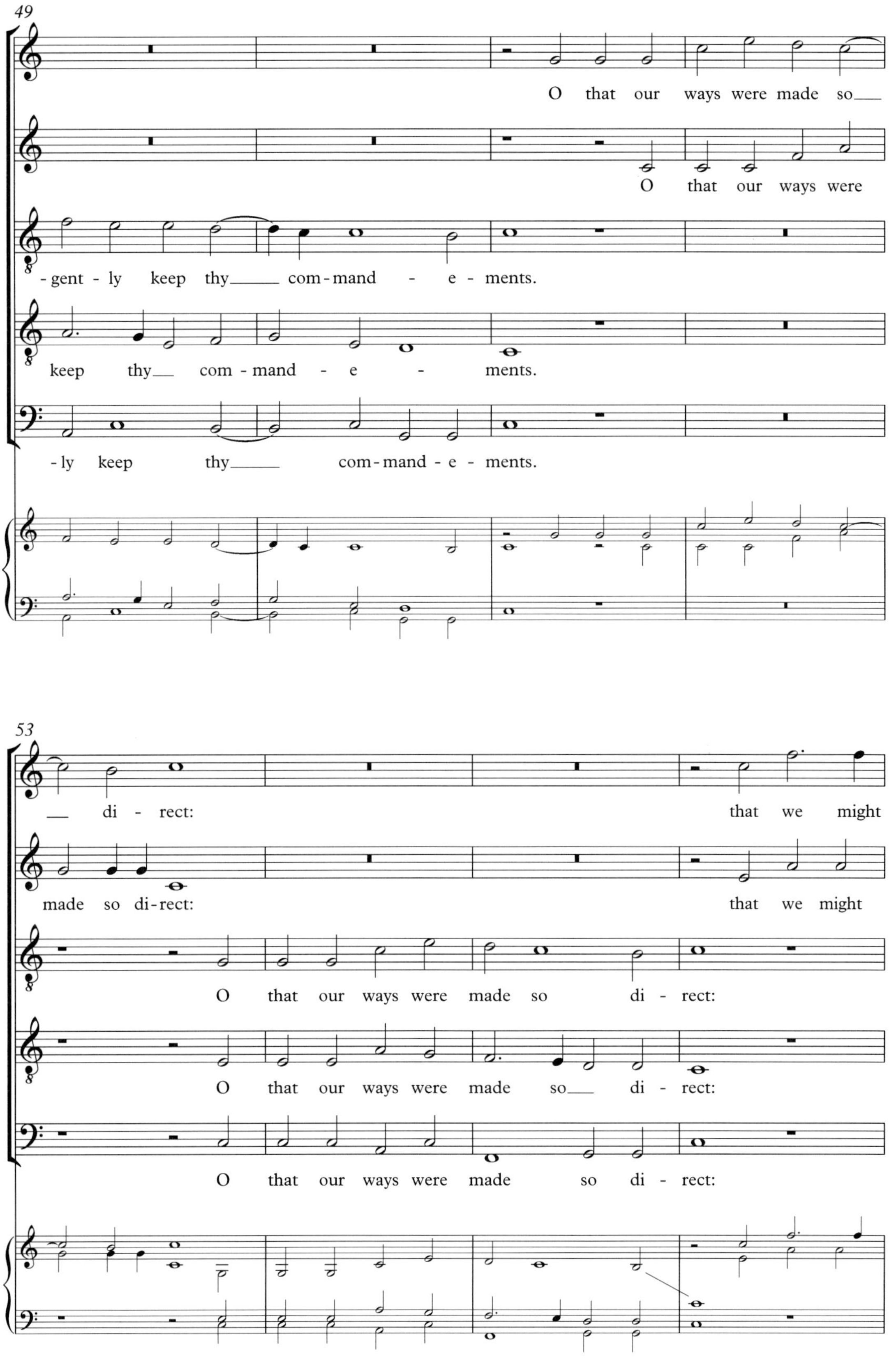

49

O that our ways were made so

O that our ways were

-gent - ly keep thy com - mand - e - ments.

keep thy com - mand - e - ments.

-ly keep thy com - mand - e - ments.

53

di - rect: that we might

made so di - rect: that we might

O that our ways were made so di - rect:

O that our ways were made so di - rect:

O that our ways were made so di - rect:

57
keep thy stat - utes.
So
keep thy stat - utes.
So
that we might keep thy stat - utes. So
that we might keep thy stat - utes.
that we might keep thy stat - utes.
61
shall we not be con-found - ed:
shall we not be con-found - ed: while we have re-spect un - to
shall we not be con - found - ed:
while we have re-

65

while we have re - spect un - to all thy

thy com - mand - e - ments, while we have re - spect un - to thy

- spect un - to all thy com - mand - ments, un - to all

68

com-mand - e - ments. Glo - ry to the Fa - ther, and

com - mand - ments. Glo - ry to the Fa - ther, and

thy com - mand - e - ments. Glo - ry to the Fa - ther, and

Glo - ry to the Fa - ther, and

Glo - ry to the Fa - ther, and

72

to the Son, and to the___ Ho - - ly Ghost.

to the___ Son, and___ to the__ Ho - ly Ghost.

to the Son, and to the Ho - - ly Ghost,

to the__ Son, and to the Ho - - ly Ghost,

to the Son, and to the Ho - - ly Ghost,

76

As it was in the be - gin - ning, is now,

As it was in the be - gin - ning, is___ now,

As it was in the be - gin - ning, is now,

As it was in the be - gin - ning, is now,

As it was in the be - gin - ning, is now, and ev -

80

and ev - er shall

and ev - er shall be, world

and ev - er shall be, world with -

and ev - er shall be, world with-out end, world

- er shall be, and ev - er shall be,

83

be, world with-out end,

with-out end, and ev -

-out end, and ev - er shall be,

with - out end, and ev - er shall be, world with-out

world with - out end, and ev - er shall be, and ev - er

87
and ev - er shall be, world with-out end.
- er shall be, world with-out end.
world with - out end.
end, world with - out end.
shall be, world with - out end.
90
A - - men. A - - - men.
A - - - - - - - - - - - men.
A - - - - - - - - - - men.
A - - - - - - - - - - - men.
A - men. A - - - - - men.

3. Hear the voice and prayer

I Kings 8: 28-30

THOMAS TALLIS
Edited by David Skinner

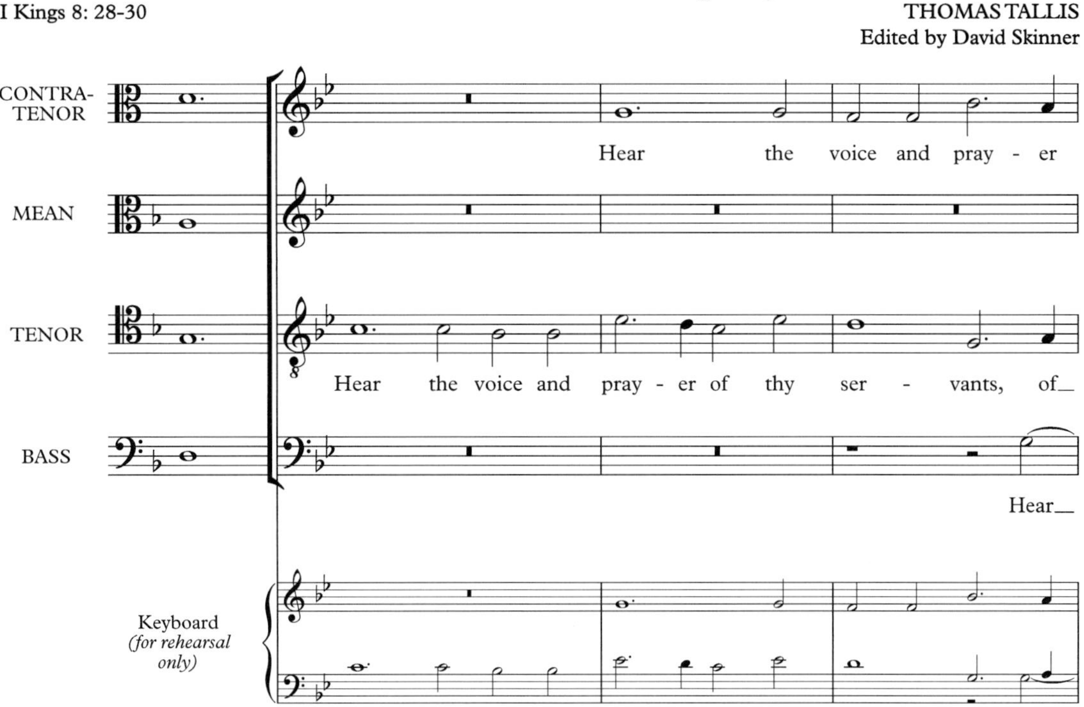

The Mean and Contratenor parts are reversed in this edition.
This anthem may also be performed down a fourth for TTBarB.

8

— that they make be - fore thee this — day.

- vants, that they make be - fore thee this day. That thine

- vants, that they make be - fore thee this day.

- vants, that they make be - fore thee this day.

12

That thine eyes may be o - pen

eyes may be o - pen to - ward this house night — and —

That thine eyes may be o - pen to-ward this house night and

That thine eyes may be o - pen to - ward this

15
to - ward this house night and day, ev - er to - ward this place, ev - er
day, this house night and day, ev - er to- ward this place, ev - er
day, night and day, ev - er to - ward this place, ev - er
house night and day, ev - er to - ward this place, ev - er
18
to - ward this place, of which thou hast said: My name shall be
to- ward this place, of
to - ward this place, of which thou hast said: My name shall be
to - ward this place, of which thou hast said: My

21

there, my name shall be there, my name shall be

which thou hast said: My name shall be there, my name shall be

there. Of which thou hast said: My name shall be

name shall be there, my name shall be there, my name shall be

24

there. And when thou hear'st, have mer-cy on them,

there. And when thou hear'st, have mer - cy on them, on them, and

there. And when thou hear'st, have mer - cy on them,

there. And when thou hear'st, have mer - cy on them,

28

and when thou hear'st, have mer - cy on them, and

when thou hear'st, and when thou hear'st, have

and when thou hear'st, have mer - cy on them, and

and when thou hear'st, have mer - cy on them, and

32

1. 2.

when thou hear'st, have mer-cy on them. them.

mer - cy on them. That thine them.

when thou hear'st, have mer-cy on them. them.

when thou hear'st, have mer - cy on them. them.

4. If ye love me

St John 14: 15-17

THOMAS TALLIS
Edited by David Skinner

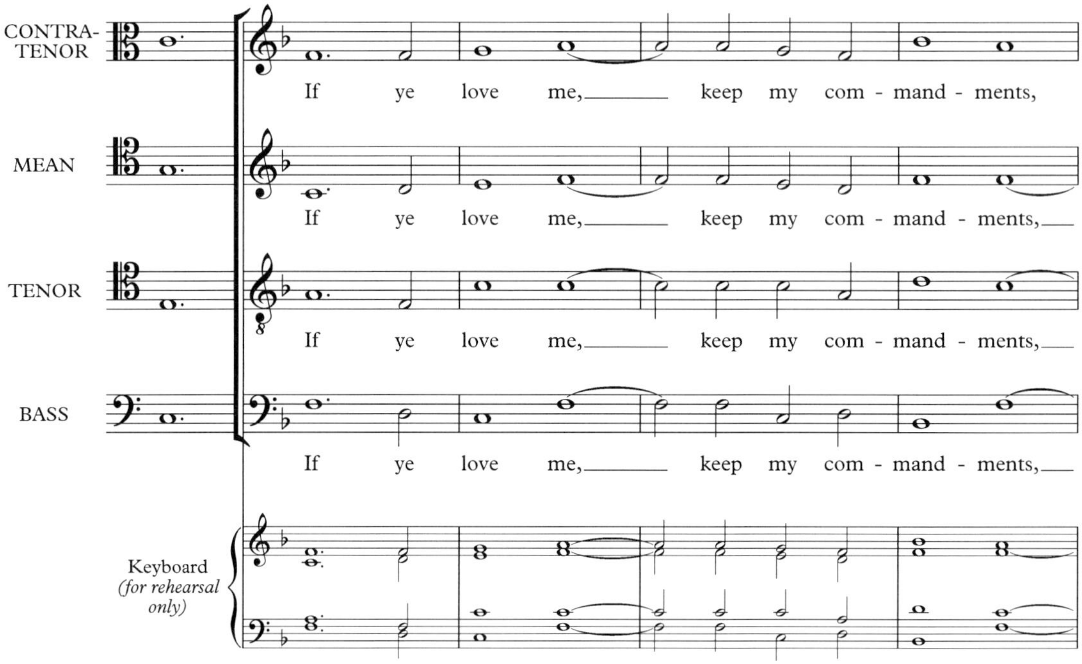

CONTRA-TENOR
If ye love me, keep my com - mand - ments,

MEAN
If ye love me, keep my com - mand - ments,

TENOR
If ye love me, keep my com - mand - ments,

BASS
If ye love me, keep my com - mand - ments,

Keyboard *(for rehearsal only)*

The Mean and Contratenor parts are reversed in this edition.
This anthem may also be performed down a fourth for TTBarB.

10
give you an - oth - er com - fort - er,
he shall give you an - oth - er com - - fort - er,
he shall give you an - oth - ther com - fort - er, that
and he shall give you an - oth - er com - fort - er,
14
that he may 'bide with you for ev -
that he may 'bide with you for ev - er, with you for ev -
he may 'bide with you for ev - er, that he may 'bide with you for ev -
that he may 'bide with you for ev - er, may 'bide with you for ev -

19
-er: e'en the spir't of truth,
-er: e'en the spir't of truth, e'en the spir't of
-er: e'en the spir't of truth, the spir't of truth, e'en
-er: e'en the spir't of truth, the spir't of truth,
23
1.
2.
e'en the spir't of truth, e'en the spir't of truth. truth.
truth, e'en the spir't of truth, e'en the spir't of truth. truth.
the spir't of truth, the spir't of truth, the spir't of truth. That truth.
e'en the spir't of truth, the spir't of truth. truth.

5. O Lord, give thy Holy Spirit

from *Lidley's Prayers*, 1566

THOMAS TALLIS
Edited by David Skinner

MEDIUS
O Lord, give thy Ho - ly Spir't in -

CONTRA-TENOR
O Lord, give thy Ho - ly Spir't in -

TENOR
O Lord, give thy Ho - ly Spir't

BASS
O Lord, give thy Ho - ly Spir't

Keyboard *(for rehearsal only)*

8
we may dwell in the fear of thy name, in the fear
we may dwell in the fear of thy name, in the fear of thy
-ing, that we may dwell in the fear of thy name,
-ing, that we may dwell in the fear of thy name,
12
of thy name, all the days of our
name, in the fear of thy name, all the days of our life,
in the fear of thy name, in the fear of thy name,
in the fear of thy name, in the fear of thy name, all

19
know thee, the on - ly true God, and Je - sus Christ
we may know thee, the on - ly true God, and Je - sus Christ
we may know thee, the on - ly true God, and
we may know thee, the on - ly true God, and Je - sus

23
whom thou hast sent, and Je - sus Christ whom thou hast sent, and
whom thou hast sent, and Je - sus Christ whom thou hast sent,
Je - sus Christ whom thou hast sent, and Je - sus Christ whom thou hast sent, and
Christ whom thou hast sent, and Je - sus Christ whom thou hast sent, and
27
1.
2.
Je - sus Christ whom thou hast sent. That we may sent.
and Je - sus Christ whom thou hast sent. That sent.
Je - sus Christ whom thou hast sent. That sent.
Je - sus Christ whom thou hast sent, hast sent. That sent.

6. O Lord, in thee is all my trust

text unknown

THOMAS TALLIS
Edited by David Skinner

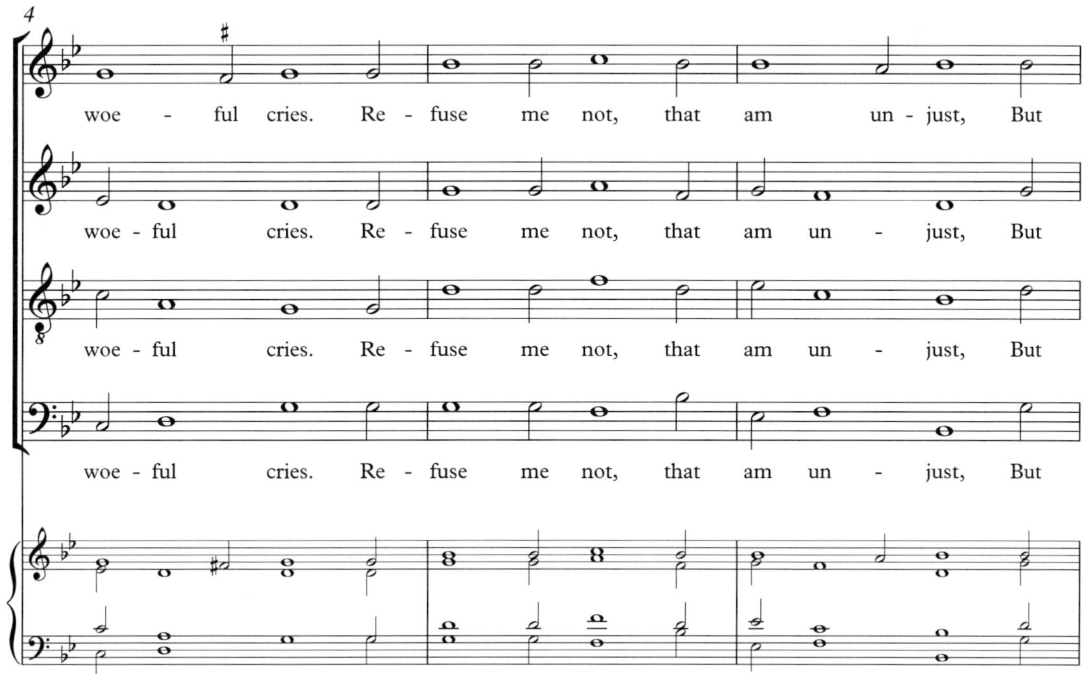

This anthem may be performed down a fourth for ATBarB.

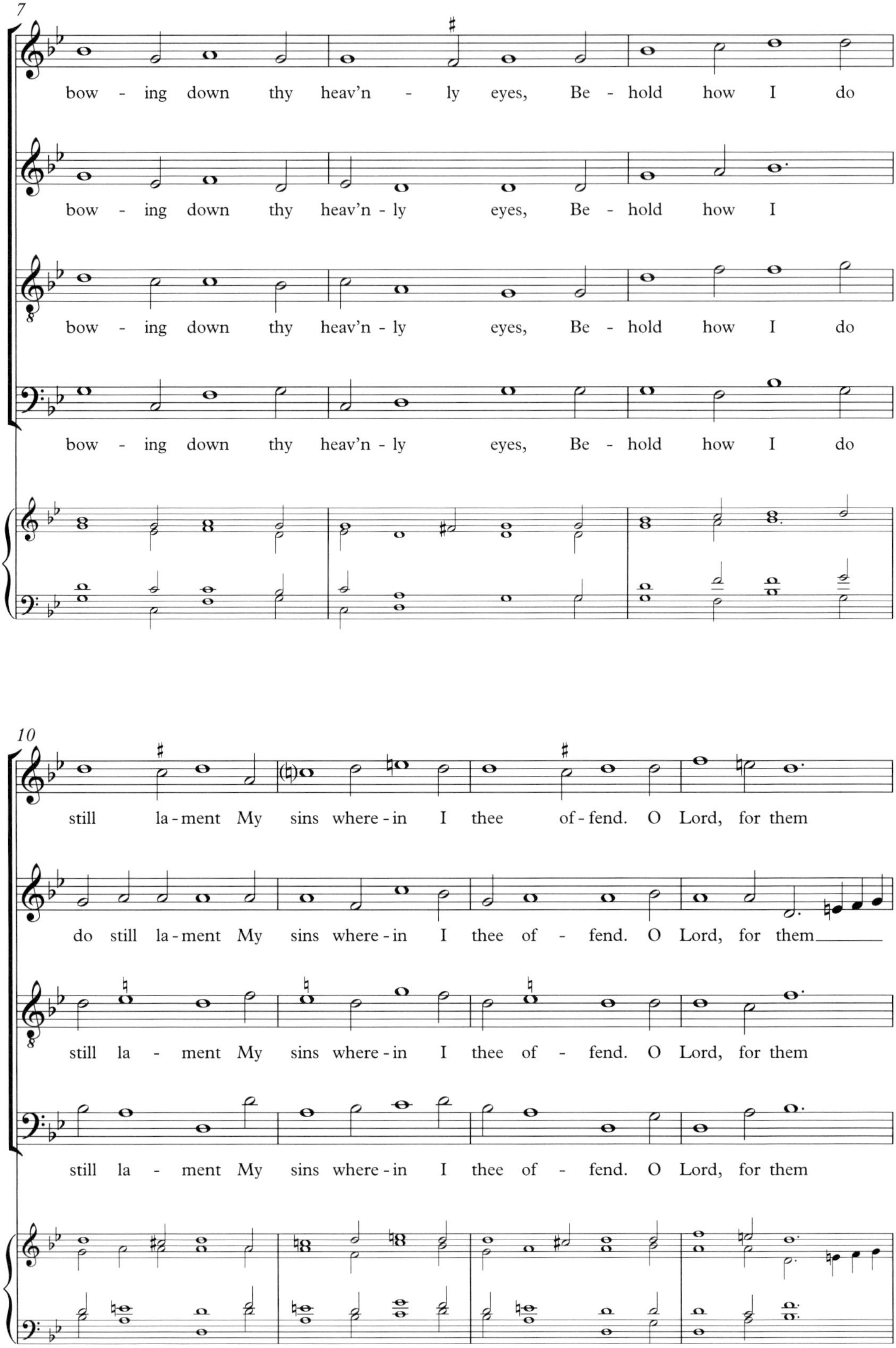

7

bow - ing down thy heav'n - ly eyes, Be - hold how I do

bow - ing down thy heav'n - ly eyes, Be - hold how I

bow - ing down thy heav'n - ly eyes, Be - hold how I do

bow - ing down thy heav'n - ly eyes, Be - hold how I do

10

still la - ment My sins where - in I thee of - fend. O Lord, for them

do still la - ment My sins where - in I thee of - fend. O Lord, for them

still la - ment My sins where - in I thee of - fend. O Lord, for them

still la - ment My sins where - in I thee of - fend. O Lord, for them

14

shall I be shent, Sith thee to please I do in - tend?

shall I be shent, Sith thee to please I do in - tend?

shall I be shent, Sith thee to please I do in - tend?

shall I be shent, Sith thee to please I do in - tend?

shent = disgraced, sith = since

17

2. No, no, not so! Thy will is__ bent To deal with sin - ners

2. No, no, not so! Thy will is bent To deal with sin - ners

2. No, no, not so! Thy will is bent To deal with sin - ners

2. No, no, not so! Thy will is bent To deal with sin - ners

20

in thine_ ire: But when in heart they shall re - pent Thou

in thine ire: But when in heart they shall re - pent Thou

in thine ire: But when in heart they shall re - pent Thou

in thine ire: But when in heart they shall re - pent Thou

23

grant'st with speed their just de - sire. To thee there - fore still

grant'st with speed their just de - sire. To thee there - fore

grant'st with speed their just de - sire. To thee there - fore still

grant'st with speed their just de - sire. To thee there - fore still

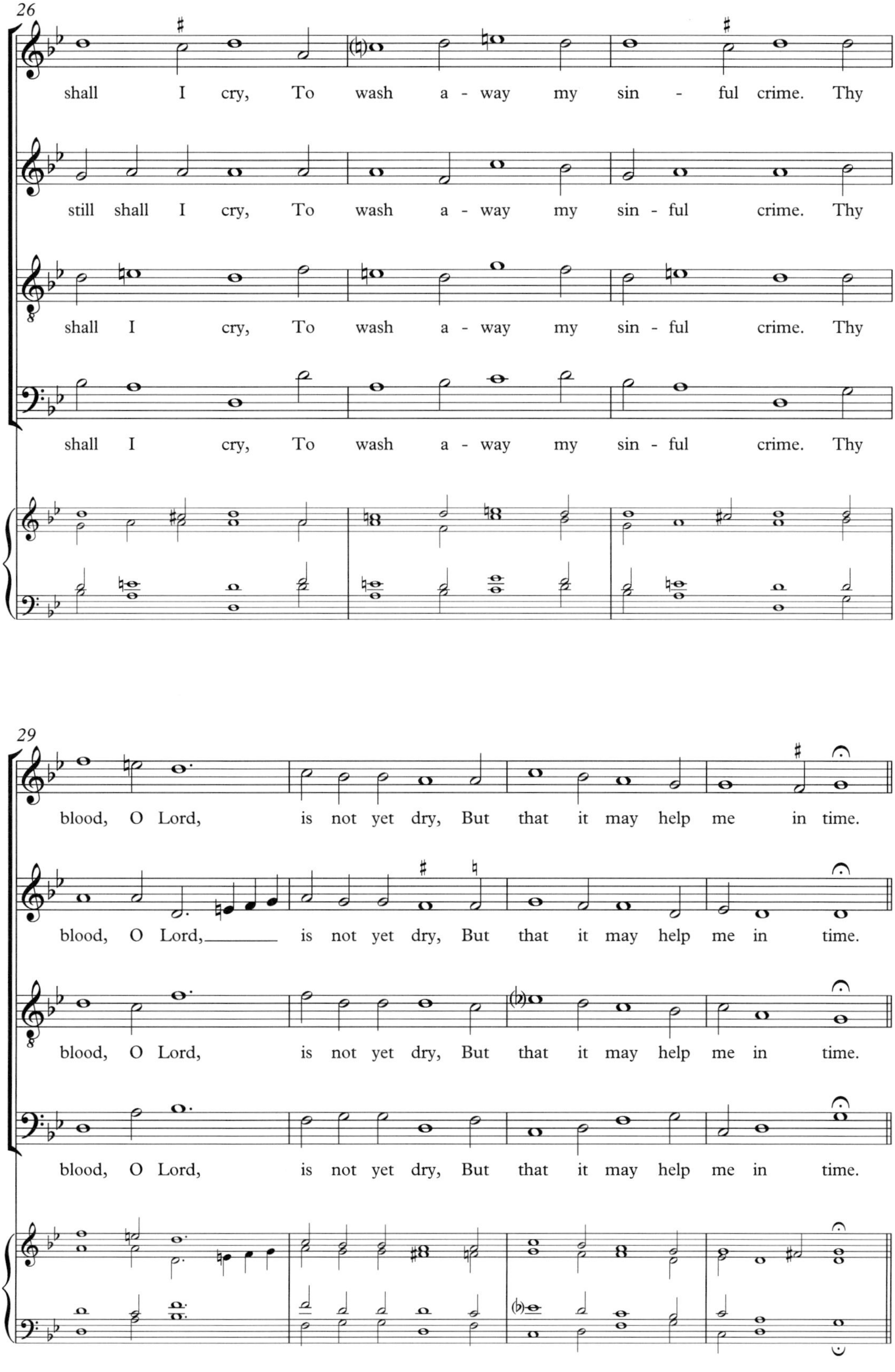

26

shall I cry, To wash a - way my sin - ful crime. Thy

still shall I cry, To wash a - way my sin - ful crime. Thy

shall I cry, To wash a - way my sin - ful crime. Thy

shall I cry, To wash a - way my sin - ful crime. Thy

29

blood, O Lord, is not yet dry, But that it may help me in time.

blood, O Lord, is not yet dry, But that it may help me in time.

blood, O Lord, is not yet dry, But that it may help me in time.

blood, O Lord, is not yet dry, But that it may help me in time.

33
3. Haste now, O Lord, haste now, I say, To pour on me the
3. Haste now, O Lord, haste now, I say, To pour on me the
3. Haste now, O Lord, haste now, I say, To pour on me the
3. Haste now, O Lord, haste now, I say, To pour on me the
36
gifts of grace, That when this life must flit a - way, In
gifts of grace, That when this life must flit a - way, In
gifts of grace, That when this life must flit a - way, In
gifts of grace, That when this life must flit a - way, In

39

heav'n with thee I may have place, Where thou dost reign

heav'n with thee I may have place, Where thou dost reign

heav'n with thee I may have place, Where thou dost reign e -

heav'n with thee I may have place, Where thou dost reign e -

42

e - ter - nal - ly, With God which once did down thee send,

e - ter - nal - ly, With God which once did down thee send,

- ter - nal - ly, With God which once did down thee send,

- ter - nal - ly, With God which once did down thee send,

45
47
Where an - gels sing con - tin - u - al - ly: To thee be praise, world
Where an - gels sing con - tin - u - al - ly: To thee be praise, world
Where an - gels sing con - tin - u - al - ly: To thee be praise, world
Where an - gels sing con - tin - u - al - ly: To thee be praise, world
48
1.
2.
with - out end. with - out end. A - - men.
with - out end. with - out end. A - - men.
with - out end. with - out end. A - - men.
with - out end. with - out end. A - - men.
1.
2.

7. Out from the deep

Psalm 130: metrical setting unknown

THOMAS TALLIS
Edited by David Skinner

8

hear my la - men - ta - ti - on.___ For if thou wilt our

hear my la - men - ta - ti - on. For if thou wilt our sins___

hear my la - men - ta - ti - on. For if thou wilt our sins be-hold,

hear my la - men - ta - ti - on.___ For

12

sins be-hold, That we have done from time to___

___ be-hold, That we have done from time to___

That we have done from time to tide, from time___

if thou wilt our sins be-hold, That we have done from time to

15
tide, O Lord, who then dare be so bold
tide, from time to tide, O Lord, who then dare be so
to tide, O Lord, who then dare be so bold, O Lord, who then dare
tide, O Lord, who then dare be so bold, O Lord, who
19
As in thy sight for to a-bide, for to a-
bold As in thy sight for to a-bide, for to a-
be so bold As in thy sight for to a-bide, for to a-
then dare be so bold As in thy sight for to a-bide, for to a-

23

-bide. For if thou wilt our sins be-hold,

-bide. For if thou wilt our sins be-hold, That

-bide. For if thou wilt our sins be-hold, That we have

-bide. For if thou wilt our

27

That we have done from time to tide,

we have done from time to tide, from

done from time to tide, from time to tide, O

sins be-hold, That we have done from time to tide, O Lord, who

30

— O Lord, who then dare be so bold As in thy

time to tide, O Lord, who then dare be so bold As

Lord, who then_ dare be so bold, O Lord, who then_ dare___ be so__

then dare be so___ bold, O Lord, who then dare be so

34

sight for to___ a-bide, for to a - - bide.

in thy sight for to___ a - bide, for___ to a - - bide.

bold As in thy sight for to a - bide, for to a - bide.

bold As in thy sight for to a - bide, for to a - bide.

8. Purge me, O Lord

text unknown

THOMAS TALLIS
Edited by David Skinner

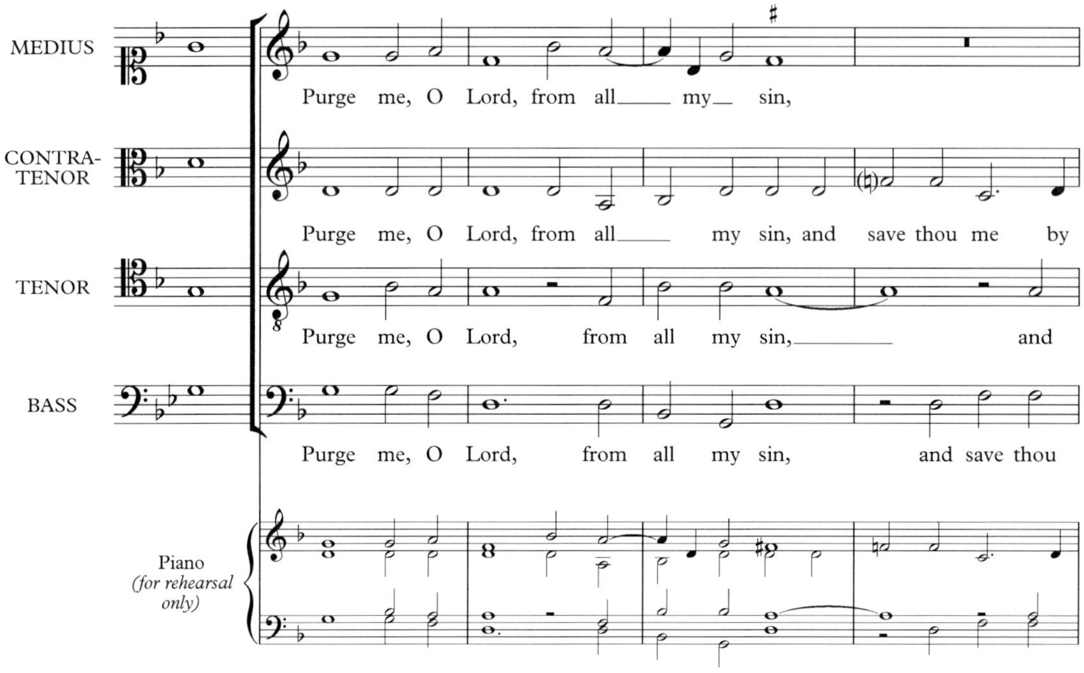
MEDIUS
Purge me, O Lord, from all my sin,
CONTRA-TENOR
Purge me, O Lord, from all my sin, and save thou me by
TENOR
Purge me, O Lord, from all my sin, and
BASS
Purge me, O Lord, from all my sin, and save thou
Piano (for rehearsal only)

5
and save thou me by faith from ill, that I may rest and
faith, and save thou me by faith from ill, that I may rest and
save thou me by faith from ill, by faith from ill, that I may rest and
me by faith from ill, that I may rest and dwell

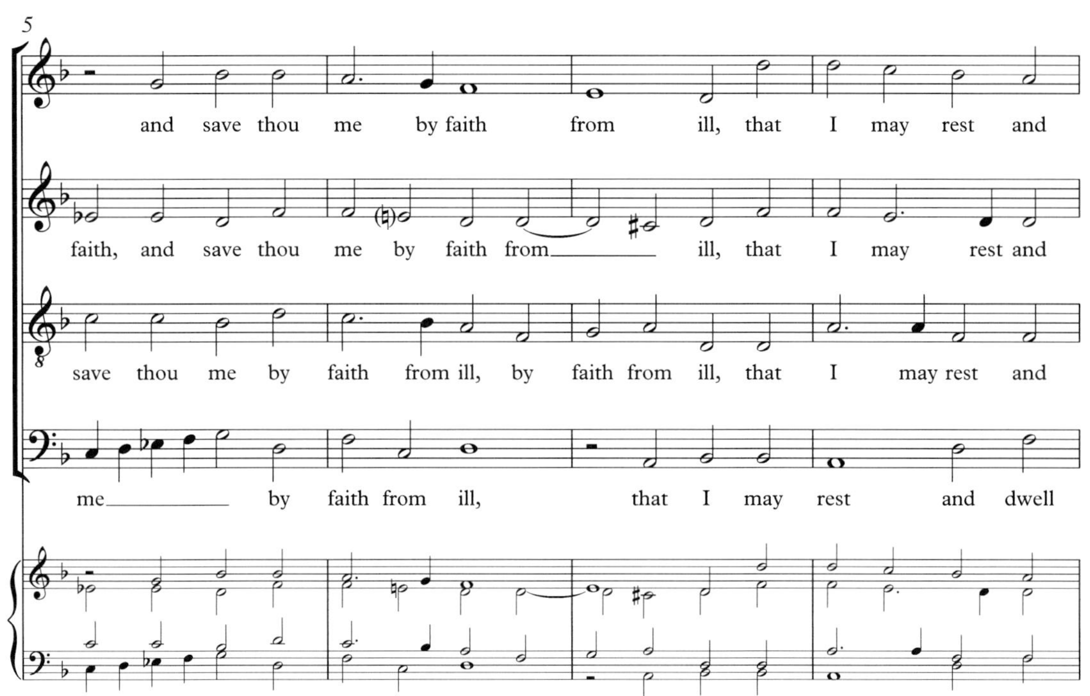

9

dwell with thee up - on thy ho - ly bless - ed hill. And

dwell with thee up - on thy ho - ly bless - ed hill. And

dwell with thee up - on thy ho - ly bless - ed hill, thy ho - ly bless - ed hill. And

with thee up - on thy ho - ly bless - ed hill, thy ho - ly bless - ed hill. And

14

that done, grant that with true heart I may with-out

that done, grant that with true* heart I may with-out hy -

that done, grant that with true heart I may with - out hy -

that done, grant that with true heart I may with -

* Bar 15, Contratenor: minims G, E.

18
hy-po - cri - sy af - firm the truth, de - tract no
-po - - cri - sy af - firm the truth, de - tract no man,
-po - cri - sy af - firm the truth, de - tract no man,
-out hy - po - cri - sy af - firm the truth, de - tract no man, but do all
22
1.
2.
man, but do all things with e - qui - ty. And — -ty.
but do all things with e - qui - ty. And — -ty.
but do all — things — with e - qui - ty. And — -ty.
things with e - qui - ty, with e - qui - ty. And — -ty.

9. Remember not, O Lord God

Psalm 79: 8-10, 14; text from the *King's Primer*, 1545

THOMAS TALLIS
Edited by David Skinner

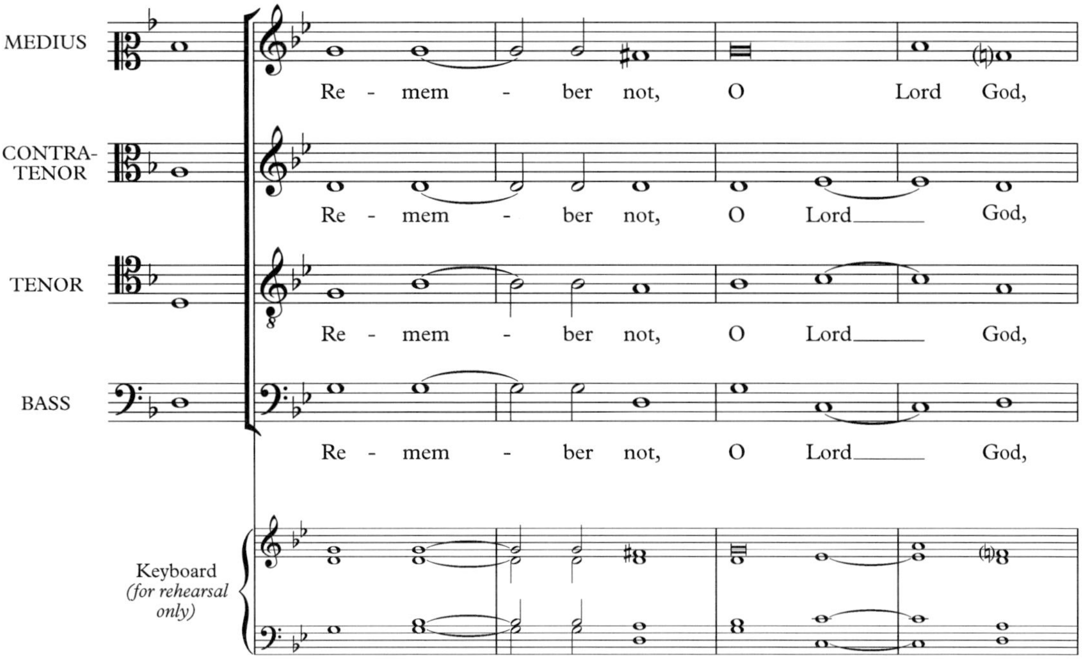

MEDIUS
Re - mem - ber not, O Lord God,

CONTRA-TENOR
Re - mem - ber not, O Lord God,

TENOR
Re - mem - ber not, O Lord God,

BASS
Re - mem - ber not, O Lord God,

Keyboard (*for rehearsal only*)

11
speed - 'ly pre - vent___ us, for we be ve - ry mis - er - a - ble,
speed - 'ly pre - vent___ us, for we be ve - ry___ mis - er - a - ble,
speed - 'ly pre - vent us, for we be ve - ry___ mis - er - a - ble,
speed - 'ly pre - vent us, for we be ve - ry___ mis - er - a - ble,
16
for we be ve - ry mis - er - a - ble, for we___ be ve - ry___
for we be ve - ry___ mis - er - a - ble, for we___ be ve - ry
for we be ve - ry mis - er - a - ble, for we___ be ve - ry
for we be ve - ry___ mis - er - a - ble, for we___ be ve - ry

21

— mis - er - a - ble. Help us, God our Sa - - vi -

mis - er - a - ble. Help us, God our Sa - vi-

mis - er - a - ble. Help us, God our Sa - vi-

mis - er - a - ble. Help us, God our Sa - vi-

26

-our, help us, God our Sa - - vi - our, and,

-our, help us, God our Sa - vi-our, and,

-our, help us, God our Sa - vi-our, and,

-our, help us, God our Sa - vi-our, and,

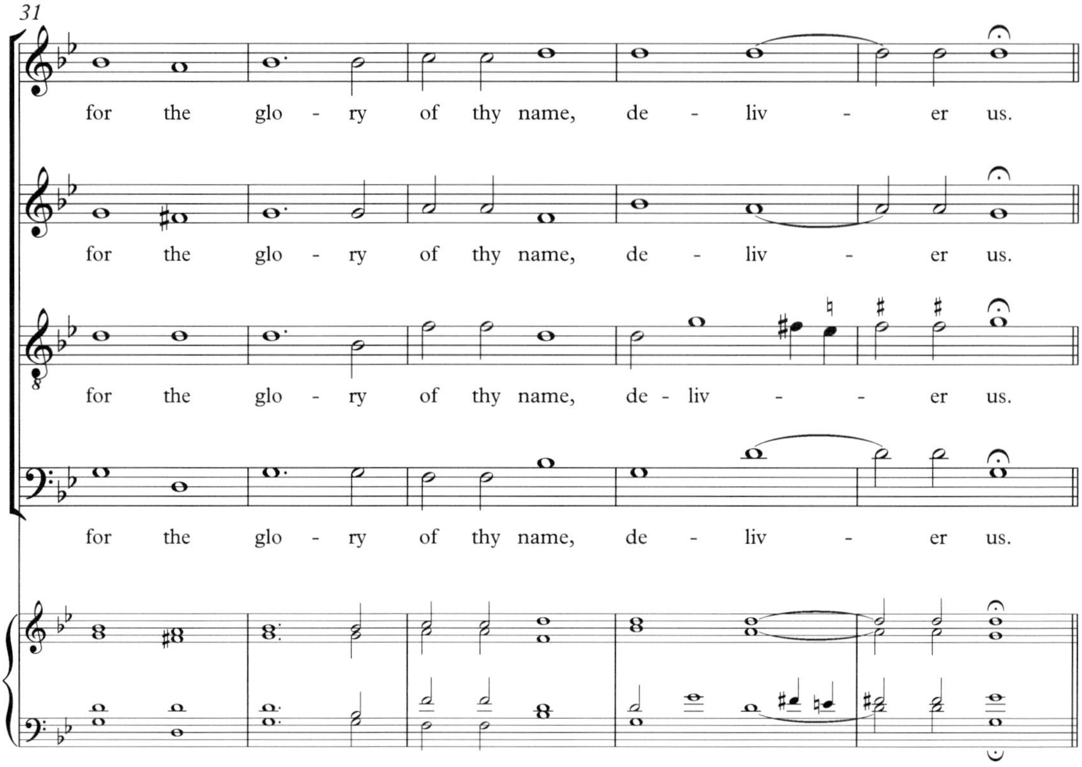

31

for the glo - ry of thy name, de - liv - er us.

for the glo - ry of thy name, de - liv - er us.

for the glo - ry of thy name, de - liv - - er us.

for the glo - ry of thy name, de - liv - er us.

36

Be mer - ci - ful and for - give our sins, for

Be mer - ci - ful and for - give our sins, for

Be mer - ci - ful and for - give our sins, for

Be mer - ci - ful and for - give our sins, for

41

thy name's___ sake, for thy name's___ sake, be mer - ci -

thy name's sake, for thy name's sake, be mer - ci -

thy name's__ sake, for thy name's__ sake, be mer - ci -

thy name's sake, for thy name's sake, be mer - ci -

46

- ful and for - give___ our___ sins, for thy name's___ sake.

- ful and for - give our___ sins, for thy name's sake.

- ful and for - give our___ sins, for thy name's__ sake.

- ful and___ for - give our sins, for thy name's sake.

51

Let not the wick - ed peo - ple say, let not the wick - ed peo - ple

Let not the wick - ed peo - ple say, let not the wick - ed peo - ple

Let not the wick - ed peo - ple say, let not the wick - ed peo - ple

Let not the wick - ed peo - ple say, let not the wick - ed peo - ple

56

say: Where is______ their God, where is______ their______ God? We

say: Where is______ their God, where is their______ God? We

say: Where is______ their______ God, where is their______ God? We

say: Where is______ their God, where is their______ God? We

61

be thy peo - ple, and the sheep of thy pas - ture. We shall

be thy peo - ple, and the sheep of thy pas - ture. We shall

be thy peo - ple, and the sheep of thy pas - ture. We shall

be thy peo - ple, and the sheep of thy pas - ture. We shall

66

give thanks un - to thee for ev - er, we shall give thanks

give thanks un - to thee for ev - er, we shall give thanks

give thanks un - to thee for ev - er, we shall give thanks

give thanks un - to thee for ev - er, we shall give thanks

71

un - to thee___ for ev - er, we shall give thanks un - to___

un - to thee___ for ev - er, we shall give thanks un - to

un - to thee___ for ev - er, we shall give thanks un - to

un - to thee___ for ev - er, we shall give thanks un - to

76

__ thee___ for ev - er. From age to age

thee for ev - er. From age to___ age

thee for ev - er. From age to age

thee for ev - er. From age to age

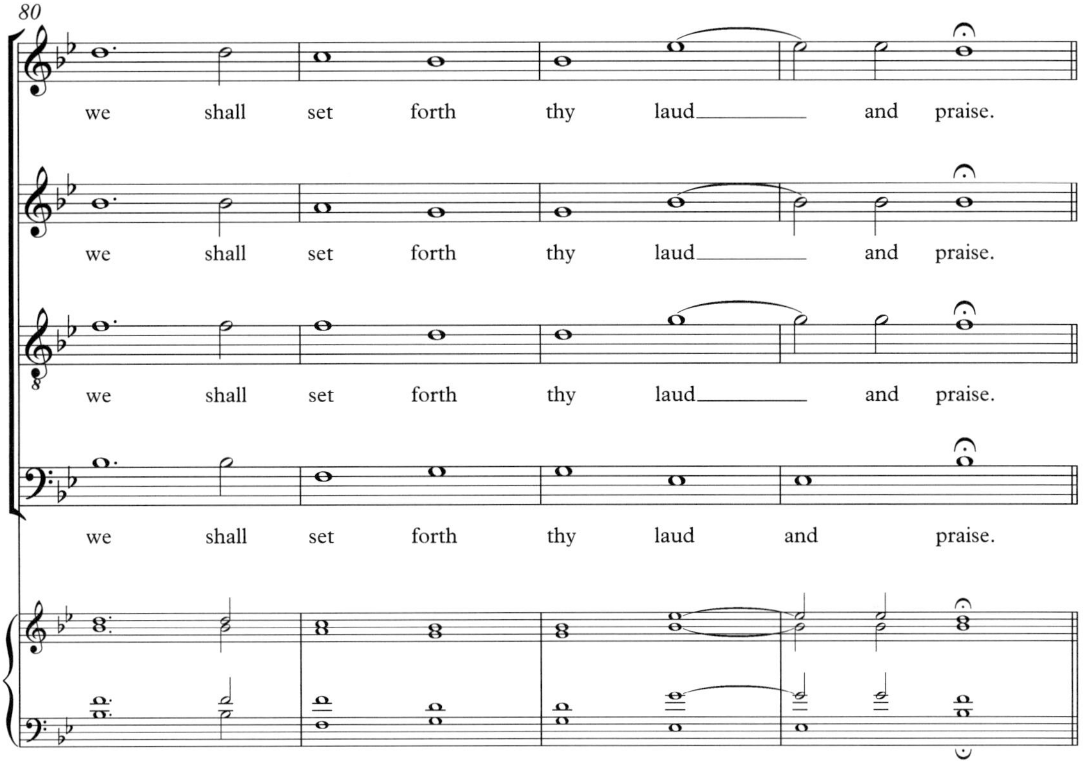

80

we shall set forth thy laud___ and praise.

we shall set forth thy laud___ and praise.

we shall set forth thy laud___ and praise.

we shall set forth thy laud and praise.

84

To thee___ be hon - our and glo - ry, to thee___

To thee___ be hon - our and glo - ry, to thee___

To thee___ be hon - our and glo - ry, to thee___

To thee___ be hon - our and glo - ry, to thee___

89

— be hon - our and glo - ry, world with - out end, world

— be hon - our and glo - ry, world with - out — end, world

— be hon - our and glo - ry, world with - out end, world

— be hon - our and glo - ry, world with - out end, world

93

with - out end, to thee be hon - our and

with - out end, to thee be hon - our and

with - out end, to thee be hon - our and

with - out end, to thee be hon - our and

97

glo - ry, world with - out end, world with - out end.

glo - ry, world with - out end, world with - out___ end.

glo - ry, world with - out end, world with - out___ end.

glo - ry, world with - out end, world with - out__ end.

101

A - - - - - - - - - men.

A - - - - - - - - - men.

A - - - - - - - - - men.

A - - - - - - - - - men.

10. Verily, verily, I say unto you

St John 6: 53-6

THOMAS TALLIS
Edited by David Skinner

MEDIUS
Ver - i - ly, ver - i - ly, I ___ say un - to you, ex -

CONTRA-TENOR
Ver - i - ly, ver - i - ly, I ___ say un - to you, ex -

TENOR
Ver - i - ly, ver - i - ly, I ___ say un - to you, ex -

BASS
Ver - i - ly, ver - i - ly, I ___ say un - to you, ex -

Keyboard *(for rehearsal only)*

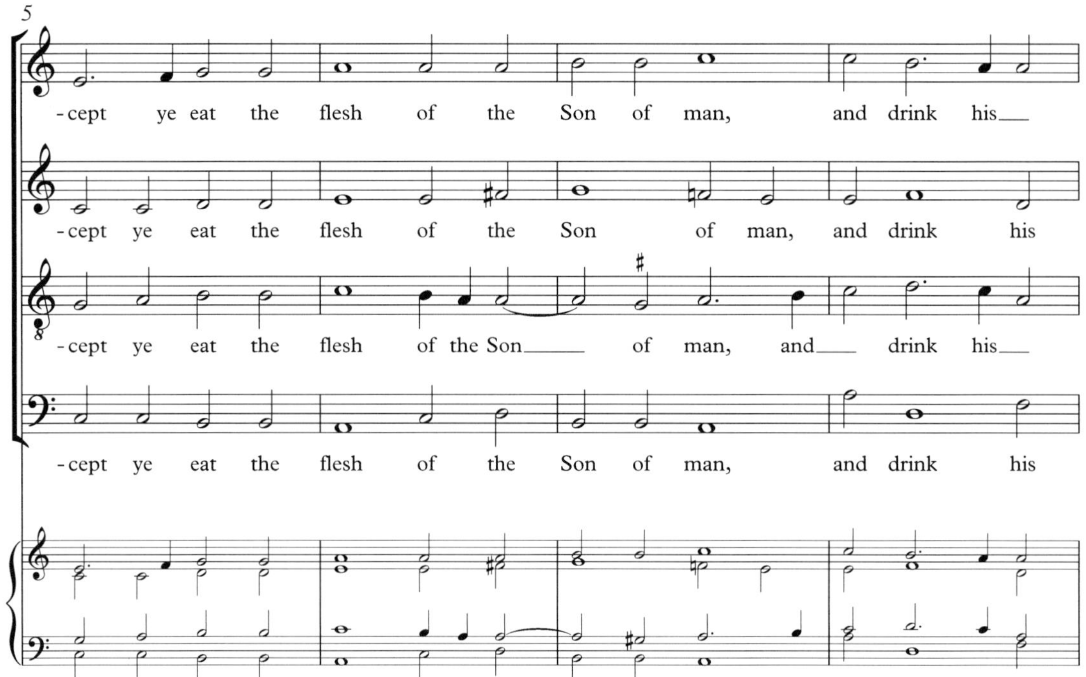

9

blood, ye have no life in______ you. Who - so eat -

blood, ye have no life in____ you. Who - so eat -

blood, ye have no life in_____ you. Who - so eat -

blood, ye have no life in you. Who - so eat -

14

-eth my flesh_____ and drink - eth my blood, hath e - ter - - -

-eth my flesh_____ and drink - eth my blood, hath e - ter - - -

-eth my flesh_____ and drink - eth my blood, hath e - ter - nal______

-eth my flesh_____ and drink - eth my blood, hath_____ e - ter -

18

- nal life; and I will raise him up at the last__ day, and I will raise him

- nal life; and I will raise him up at the last day, and I will

__ life; and I will raise him up at the last day, and I will

-nal life; and I will raise him up at the last day, and I will raise him

22

up at the last day. For my flesh is meat in - deed,

raise him up at the last day. For my flesh is meat in - deed,

raise him up at the last day. For my flesh is meat in - deed,

up at the last day. For my flesh is meat in - deed,

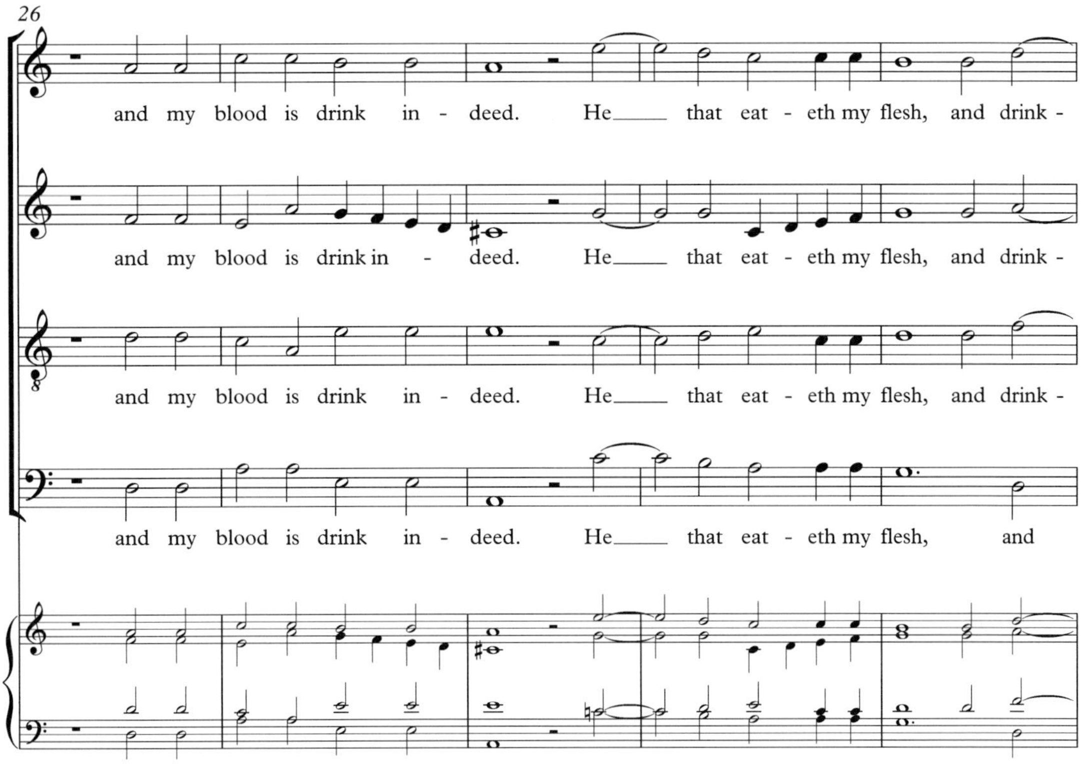

26

and my blood is drink in - deed. He___ that eat - eth my flesh, and drink -

and my blood is drink in - deed. He___ that eat - eth my flesh, and drink -

and my blood is drink in - deed. He___ that eat - eth my flesh, and drink -

and my blood is drink in - deed. He___ that eat - eth my flesh, and

31

- eth my___ blood, dwell - eth in me, and I___ in___ him.

- eth my blood, dwell - eth in me, and I in him.

- eth my___ blood, dwell - eth in me, and I in him.

drink - eth my blood, dwell - eth in me, and I in him.

1 2 3 4 5 6 7 8 9